Designer Bead Embroidery

Designer Bead Embroidery

150 PATTERNS AND COMPLETE TECHNIQUES

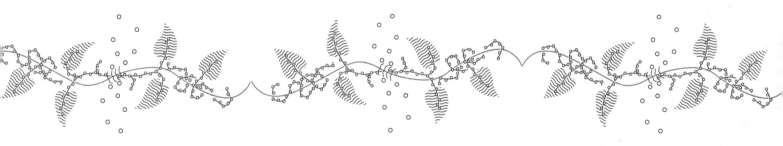

Kenneth D. King

Creative Publishing
international

First published in 2006 in the
US and Canada by:

Creative Publishing international, Inc.

**Creative Publishing
international**

18705 Lake Drive East
Chanhassen, Minnesota 55317
1-800-328-3895
www.creativepub.com

Library of Congress CIP Data

King, Kenneth D.
  Designer bead embroidery : 150 patterns and
complete techniques / Kenneth D. King.
    p. cm.
ISBN-13: 978-1-58923-272-3 (soft cover)
  ISBN-10: 1-58923-272-0 (soft cover)
  1. Bead embroidery. I. Title.
TT860.K56 2006
746.5--dc22   2006012722

QUAR.EBB

Copyright © Quarto Inc. 2006
Conceived, designed, and produced by
Quarto Publishing Inc.
The Old Brewery
6 Blundell Street
London N7 9BH

Senior Editor: **Jo Fisher**
Art Editor and Designer: **Elizabeth Healey**
Text Editor: **Tracie Davis**
Photographers: **Martin Norris
& Kenneth D. King**
Illustrator: **John Woodcock**
Assistant Art Director: **Penny Cobb**
Art Director: **Moira Clinch**
Publisher: **Paul Carslake**

Manufactured by Modern Age Repro House Ltd,
Hong Kong
Printed by SNP Leefung Printer Ltd, China
10 9 8 7 6 5 4 3 2 1

Contents

HOW TO USE THIS BOOK

The first section, Equipment and Techniques, contains information about all of the tools, equipment, beads, and fabrics that are traditionally used in bead embroidery. Key techniques, such as transferring patterns to fabric and how to use frames and hoops, are explained, along with step-by-step illustrations. A Stitch Library is included, which demonstrates the basic stitches that you will need to master in order to create your beaded embroidery.

The Designs section contains 150 inspirational designs, complete with full instructions and schematic pattern illustrations that you can enlarge and copy. The different categories of design include borders, edgings, and fills, and you can mix and match these to achieve exactly the composition you desire. Each design lists all the beads and stitches used in its execution.

Reduced-down photograph of finished piece. If you want to work with actual-size photographs, divide either the height or width of the actual dimensions (given in pattern instructions) by the height or width of the reduced-down photograph. Multiply the total by 100. For example, Wedding Daisy measures 5¼ x 3¼ in (13.5 x 8.5cm). Its photograph measures 2⅝ x 1⁹⁄₁₆ in (6.7 x 4cm). (5¼ (13.5) ÷ 2⅝ (6.7)) x 100 = 201%. Use a photocopier to enlarge the photograph by 201%.

List of the stitches used to make the piece (see the Stitch Library, pages 34–39, for full instructions for each stitch)

Enlargement ratio: enlarge the pattern illustration on a photocopier by this percentage to achieve the actual size

Pattern

Instructions for completing each pattern. Includes dimensions of the finished piece and a description of possible uses and applications.

List of beads used to make the piece. Includes a photograph of each bead, a code number (below each photograph) referring you to the Bead Index on pages 120–125 for a full bead description, and the amount (either in grams or number of beads) you will require.

86 Designs

WEDDING DAISY

Embellishments

15g — 117
5g — 60
11 — 148
5g — 9

Stitches
~~~ Satin stitch
o-o-o Sequins on a running stitch
∿∿∿ Bouclé stitch

🔍 Enlarge pattern by 188%

Dimensions 5¼ x 3¼ in (13.5 x 8.5cm)
Applications This simple daisy is perfect for the bride whose beauty is her jewel. Use it in repetition to trim the hem of a simple empire-style gown, and then pair this with a headdress of fresh daisies.
Method Fill in the petals with sequins, working from the tips to the center, using sequins on a running stitch. Next, stitch on the circle of 8mm roses montées, and fill this circle with 6/0 iridescent gold seed beads using bouclé stitch (3 beads per stitch). Finally, fill in the stem and leaves with 11/0 two-cut beads in satin stitch.

Introduction

This book has grown out of an exploration I began over 20 years ago. When I first started out as a designer, I wanted to make beaded evening clothes and accessories. At the time, there were no good books on the subject. Since I had lots of time, and not much ready cash, I decided to teach myself beading.

I studied as many examples as I could get my hands on, and made many things that ended up in the landfill, but came out of this exploration with a base of knowledge that serves me to this day. When my design business took off, I got a reputation for my beautifully and opulently embellished clothing and accessories that eventually sold to the rich and famous. Later, I was asked to teach a class on beaded embellishment at The Sewing Workshop in San Francisco. Word got around, and now I find myself teaching seminars on bead embroidery all across North America.

This book covers only embroidering with beads—sewing beads to a base fabric with needle and thread. There are other ways to work with beads, such as machine sewing, tambour hook, and glue, but those methods are not covered here.

In addition, I have only specified readily available materials. When I started out, I lived in San Francisco and had limited access to exotic materials. I also couldn't afford some of the more pricey beads, so I learned how to make the more garden-variety things that I could afford look better and richer than they actually were.

This book provides you with all the information and inspiration you need—the instructions and the designs contained here may be applied to whatever type of beautiful beaded article or garment you decide to create.

Know that these motifs are just a starting point. They can be duplicated, re-interpreted in different colors, or experimented with in many other ways. Remember—you are the designer and the look you desire is paramount. Use this book simply as a base from which to express yourself.

Kenneth D. King

CHAPTER 1
EQUIPMENT AND TECHNIQUES

This chapter introduces all the tools and materials required to begin creating luxurious beaded pieces. Embroidering with beads doesn't require any expensive investment: the tools are small and easy to find, and the materials—beads, threads, and fabrics—are readily available and come in a variety of price ranges.

In addition, important beading techniques are demonstrated and design considerations, such as beading placement and color choices, are discussed.

BEADS, SEQUINS, AND STONES

Beads, sequins, and stones come in an astonishing variety of colors, sizes, and shapes. Whenever possible, use glass beads and stones, as these will look better and last over time. Sequins are usually made from plastic, but the quality of the plastic varies. When purchasing these items, price is one way to determine quality. However, you need not break the bank—do a visual inspection to check for uniformity of color and size. Finally, buy things you love—whether it is inexpensive or not, if you love it you will use it. Buying materials that don't "speak" to you makes them more expensive, as they will sit in your stash forever.

BEADS

Beads are generally symmetrical along a central axis, and have a hole vertically down that axis or across a narrow end. The most common beads are seed beads (also known as caviar beads), bugle beads (tubular in shape), and "cut" beads, but there are many other varieties available.

Seed beads Also known as rocaille beads, seed beads are somewhat round (not perfect spheres), and roughly as long as they are wide. They come in different sizes, from very tiny to very large (known as "crow beads").

Cut beads Similar in size to seed beads and made out of the same materials and finishes, cut beads have flat surfaces cut or molded into the bead. "Two-cut" beads look like hexagons when viewed on the hole side of the bead. In vintage beadwork, "jet" embroidery made use of lots of black cut beads.

Bugle beads Bugle beads are tubular in shape and can be either perfectly cylindrical, made with flat sides, or what are called "twisted" bugles. They are made in lengths from 1/8 in (2mm) up to 1 1/2 in (40mm) long, at which point they are called glass tubes. Something to be mindful of with bugle beads is how they are cut to length. The less expensive beads are broken to length, which makes the edges of the holes extremely sharp. This will result in cut threads over time. Better quality beads have fire-polished holes.

Round These beads are spherical in shape, and sold by diameter size. They can be glass, plastic, or metal. Costume pearls fall into this category. Costume pearls can be glass or plastic, the glass ones being the higher quality, but they are all prone to damage by scratching or abrasion.

Roundel These beads are donut-shaped, which means they are wider than they are tall. They are made in different materials: plastic, glass, metal, and rhinestone-set.

Drops or pendant beads These are narrow at one end and wide at the other. The hole is either drilled vertically down the length of the bead, or horizontally across the narrow end.

Lozenge These beads are either an elongated rectangle, or diamond shape, with a hole drilled down the length of the bead.

Faceted These beads can be round, roundel, drop, or lozenge shapes, but are beads that have flat surfaces cut into them. There are two types: fire-polished and cut. The Swarovski brand is the finest example of cut beads—they are made of fine lead crystal, and the edges of the facets are crisp, because the beads are cut like gems. They are expensive but are worth the price if you want a first-rate result.

● Seed bead   ▬ Cut bead   ▮ Bugle bead   ● Round   ◉ Roundel   ◗ Drop   ◆ Lozenge

SEQUINS

Sequins are generally flat or have a low relief to them. Those commonly known as sequins are disc-shaped with a hole punched in the center—these can be flat or cup-shaped. Paillettes are disc-shaped sequins with the hole punched at the edge. The rest can be called "novelty"—there is a broad variety of shapes available.

Sequins These are round and either completely flat or slightly cup-shaped, with a hole in the center. Cup sequins are domed in the center, with a smooth or slightly faceted surface.

Paillettes These are round sequins with the hole punched at the edge.

Novelty A catch-all category that includes all fancy shapes, from leaves and flowers, to marquise, navette (boat) shape, stars, animals, lozenge, and crescent moons. You can even use watch gears as sequins.

Findings These are not sequins but they are included here because they do relate to sequins. Findings (also called stampings) are metal (gold- or silver-colored) shapes and objects produced for making jewelry, such as bells, filigree, insects—the choices are endless. They generally have holes drilled in them, so you can sew them down. One or two of these can really make the centerpiece of a motif.

STONES

Stones are often the focal points of a composition. They are available in a variety of shapes, but are distinguished by the method of attachment. Stones are either flat-backed with holes drilled through the glass, or claw-backed (roses or chaton montées), which means they are mounted into a metal fitting.

Flat-back These stones come in a variety of shapes and sizes, but the common factor is that they have a flat, silvered back, and at least one hole drilled into the stone for attaching to the fabric.

Lochrosen This is a subset of the flat-back stone, usually made by Swarovski. They are round, and look like a thick, faceted crystal sequin, with a hole in the center. They come in different sizes, and in either plain or AB (aurore boreale) finish.

Claw-back These stones are not drilled, but set into a pronged metal mounting. The stones themselves can be either flat-back or point-back, but they are mounted in metal and the metal is sewn to the fabric. Again, they come in a variety of shapes and sizes, and as usual, price determines quality, with Swarovski (roses or chaton montées) being the best.

Looking after your beads

◎ Before using beads, sequins, and stones, consider how the finished item will be cleaned, and test your beads with any process they will be exposed to, before you begin your project. This will eliminate any unpleasant surprises that might occur, because the materials were not compatible with the processes you used to produce or care for the piece.

◎ Some beads are dyed and water can make the color bleed. Avoid using these beads on items that will be hand-washed.

◎ Dry-cleaning can cloud or completely dissolve sequins, and can remove some bead finishes, such as the coating on costume pearls.

◎ Some sequins will warp, shrink, or cloud over, if exposed to steam, so should not be used on items that will be steam-pressed.

Faceted   *Sequin*   *Novelty*   *Finding*   *Flat-back*   *Lochrosen*   *Claw-back*

FABRIC AND THREADS

No matter how beautiful your beads, sequins, and stones might be, for a successful project you need good fabric and threads. Some people insist on silk fabrics and natural fiber threads, but this is not necessary. With the improvement of man-made fibers today, you can choose a microfiber fabric that has the same luster and feel as a natural fiber. The advantage of man-made fibers is their longevity—a piece made on polyester will last longer than one made on natural fiber. This same bias toward man-made fibers extends to threads as well—they will last far longer than their natural counterparts.

Monofilament

Polyester thread

Metallic polyester thread

Nymo thread

Thread color

When choosing thread color, the rule of thumb is to match the background fabric. The exception is when making a stop stitch or stitches where the thread will show between the beads. In those cases, you should match the bead color. When in doubt, make a sample to see which color looks best.

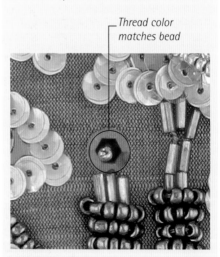

Thread color matches bead

THREAD

Just as you wouldn't use the same sewing needle in your machine for every type of fabric, you will want to use different threads for different purposes. When choosing thread, consider factors such as appearance (matching color to the fabric), strength (will the piece need to withstand heavy wear?), method of cleaning, and longevity.

Polyester or cotton-wrapped polyester
Polyester is impervious to moisture, and is strong and flexible. Cotton-wrapped polyester or 100 percent polyester thread is ideal for most work.

Nymo This is nylon thread that looks like dental floss. It has a high tensile strength, does not stretch, and comes in different sizes. Nymo thread is ideal for beading onto areas that will withstand heavy wear such as cuffs and elbows.

Silamide This two-ply twisted nylon thread can be used in the same way as Nymo thread. The fiber is the same as that used for bulletproof vests, and is very strong. Knots have a tendency to come undone, so be extra careful when tying

off, or put on a dot of an anti-fray product or seam sealant to avoid this.

Monofilament This is a transparent nylon thread that comes in different diameters. Fine monofilament thread is useful for edging veiling with seed beads, but using it to embroider beads is troublesome, and it is not as strong as a good polyester thread.

Tigertail A very fine metal cable coated with clear plastic, tigertail is usually used for stringing bead necklaces, but can be used for couching beads or for fringes, though it is more expensive than monofilament.

Piano wire Also known as "craft wire," this is a fine wire used for couching beads such as long bugles that have holes that would cut through the thread. When using piano wire, string the beads onto the wire, and then couch the strand down to the fabric.

Tigertail

Organza (in background)

Chiffon

Crepe

Velvet

FABRICS

You can embroider on any kind of fabric, so the choice is personal, but there are some fabrics that are traditionally used for bead embroidery.

Organza The best fabric for making appliqués is organza, because it is lightweight and transparent. Polyester organza is ideal because it will last over time. If you are embroidering onto organza for a garment, you will need to line the garment with a second layer of organza to finish the back of the embroidery.

Chiffon Much lovely embroidery is seen on chiffon. As with organza, you should line the chiffon with a second layer of chiffon to finish the back of the work.

Crepe and charmeuse These drapey fabrics look well with bead embroidery. It is not necessary to use silk these days, because with new microfibers you can have the look of silk but the strength and practicality of man-made fiber.

Velvet The nap on velvet presents a challenge. When marking the fabric for the frame, you need plenty of extra fabric around the work, as the stress you will put on the edges of the fabric when stretching it into the frame will crush the nap. If the nap of the velvet is especially deep, make padded satin stitch (see page 35) when filling areas with solid beading. This padding will keep the beads above the surface of the nap, so they won't get lost. Because velvet is expected to feel deep and luxurious, a layer of batting and organza sandwiched behind the velvet before working will give the whole piece a quilted, full look.

Knits It is possible to embroider on knits, but the stretch of the knit is an issue. You can stabilize the back of a beaded area with a woven fabric (organza is good for this, as it doesn't add weight). Another way to stabilize a beaded knit is to line the garment with a woven fabric such as China silk—beaded cardigans from the 1950s are good examples of this method.

Beading stretch fabric

Spaced repetitive patterns such as a step-and-repeat on knits cause problems. You don't want to carry the thread under the fabric from one repeat to another, so you will need to knot off each portion of the pattern and cut the thread. This will enable the knit to stretch normally, which is especially important if you are making dance or skating costumes, which are usually made of stretch fabrics. Make sure all beads on these costumes are secure. If a bead falls off during a performance, it is a safety hazard!

Knits

EQUIPMENT

The success of any project depends partly upon having the proper tools and equipment to do the job efficiently. Happily, the equipment needed for bead embroidery is not terribly expensive or hard to find. Some items, such as scissors and embroidery hoops and frames, can be bought at any embroidery supplier, or from the notions counter at your fabric store. Other items are tools you may already have in your home, or things that you can make yourself.

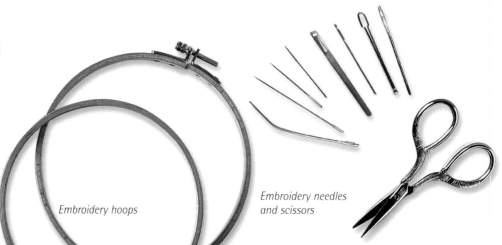

Embroidery scroll frame

Sewing machine A sewing machine is used to hem edges of the fabric for the embroidery frame, and also to pierce the paper when making a pounce pattern (see pages 26–27).

Steam iron A steam iron is needed to steam the back of finished work to "set" the stitches. Any household steam iron will do, and as you won't touch the fabric with it, use the "wool" setting.

Embroidery hoop Hoops are used for embroidering small motifs or to make appliqués. You can use any size, but one that is 12 in (30cm) in diameter is the most useful.

Embroidery scroll frame These frames hold the fabric taut as you work. They can be purchased at any store that carries embroidery supplies. If possible, purchase one with a stand, as this will make working much easier.

Bead containers You can purchase clear plastic containers specifically designed to store beads. Small ziplock bags and plastic film canisters can also be used.

Bead holders When working a frame, you want lightweight, flat bead containers. You can make your own out of felt—roll-hem a rectangle of felt and sew tucks across it to separate the beads.

Scissors A good pair of embroidery scissors is useful for trimming threads. You should also have a pair of inexpensive "snips" for cutting thread to length—this will save wear on your embroidery scissors.

Beading needles These are long, thin needles that come in sizes 10 to 13. Size 10 is the thickest and 13 the thinnest. A size 12 needle fits through most beads.

Sketchpad Any sketchpad will do for most designing, but newsprint is not recommended. It deteriorates over time, so any designs you draw on it won't last.

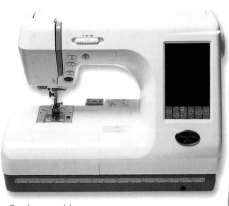

Sewing machine

Embroidery hoops

Embroidery needles and scissors

Artist's pencil

Organizing your materials is a great way to inspire creativity. Containers such as this partitioned clear plastic case serve to both organize, and make your materials easily visible.

Artist's pencil The soft lead of an artist's pencil works best for marking fabrics, especially organza for appliqué.

Pounce bag and white kraft paper These are used to make pounce patterns. The kraft paper is sturdy enough to make a good pattern after the piercing (see pages 26–27), and the pounce bag holds the power that marks the fabric.

Brush Needed for brushing fabric—any brush will work for this purpose, but an inexpensive soft-bristle paintbrush (called a "chip" brush) works best. Make sure to cover the brush's metal mount with fabric to guard against snagging your work. A stencil brush will remove stubborn chalk marks from fabric—again, cover the metal mount with fabric.

Lamp A good light is essential for working on delicate embroidery. It will help you avoid eyestrain and the fatigue that comes with it. The "Ott-Lite®" is the most popular kind of working light.

Tip

Carry a beading needle with you when you are buying beads so you can test to see if they are large enough for the needle to pass through. There is nothing more frustrating than to buy beads that are too small for the needle.

Chip brush with covered handle

Home-made portable bead tray

DESIGNING WITH BEADS

There are no definite rules when designing a work, but having some guidelines drawn from precedent is helpful in getting started. Beading, when used, needs some reason for being there—otherwise it can look like an afterthought.

In surveying a variety of garments drawn from a number of sources, there are some definite trends that can be seen. On the following pages, these trends are separated into categories. Note that there can be overlap in the different categories, with some pieces using elements from more than one.

A SIMPLE EDGING

Autumn Leaves (page 80)

Edgings are a good way to add a luxurious touch to a scarf or belt. Embroider separately on organza and add onto the scarf, as for this motif, or work directly onto the fabric.

This border is worked as four sections of appliqué onto two layers of organza. After you work the sections, sew them together with mitered corners, then add the necessary beads over the seams to connect the motifs. Stitch the border to the scarf in the same way as a facing.

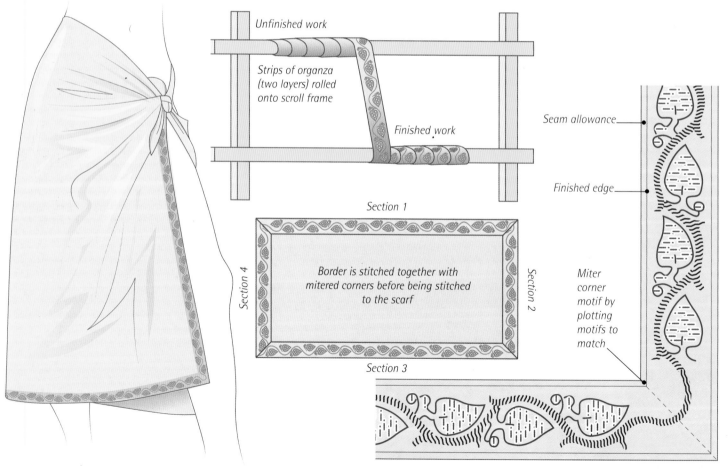

Unfinished work

Strips of organza (two layers) rolled onto scroll frame

Finished work

Section 1

Section 4

Border is stitched together with mitered corners before being stitched to the scarf

Section 2

Section 3

Seam allowance

Finished edge

Miter corner motif by plotting motifs to match

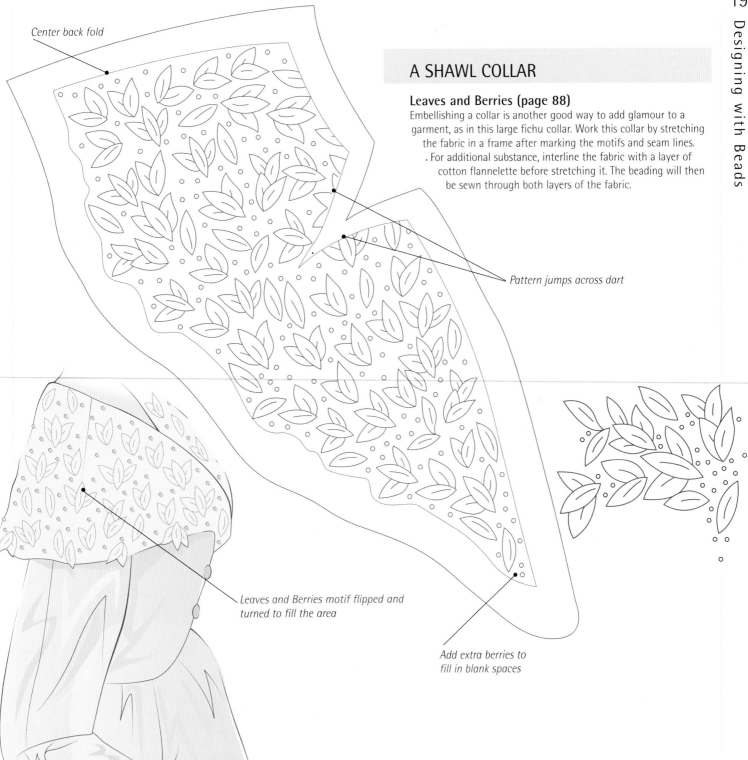

Center back fold

A SHAWL COLLAR

Leaves and Berries (page 88)

Embellishing a collar is another good way to add glamour to a garment, as in this large fichu collar. Work this collar by stretching the fabric in a frame after marking the motifs and seam lines. . For additional substance, interline the fabric with a layer of cotton flannelette before stretching it. The beading will then be sewn through both layers of the fabric.

Pattern jumps across dart

Leaves and Berries motif flipped and turned to fill the area

Add extra berries to fill in blank spaces

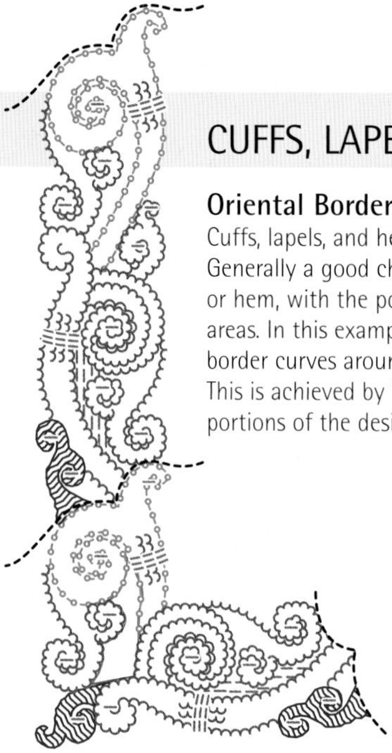

CUFFS, LAPELS, AND HEMS

Oriental Border (page 74)

Cuffs, lapels, and hems are good focal points for beadwork on a garment. Generally a good choice of design would be a border to edge the cuff, lapel, or hem, with the possible addition of other motifs to fill the remaining areas. In this example, an elaborate border has been chosen. Notice how the border curves around the edge of the jacket, and around the lapel facing. This is achieved by "walking" the border around the curve, tracing out portions of the design as you edge it around the curve.

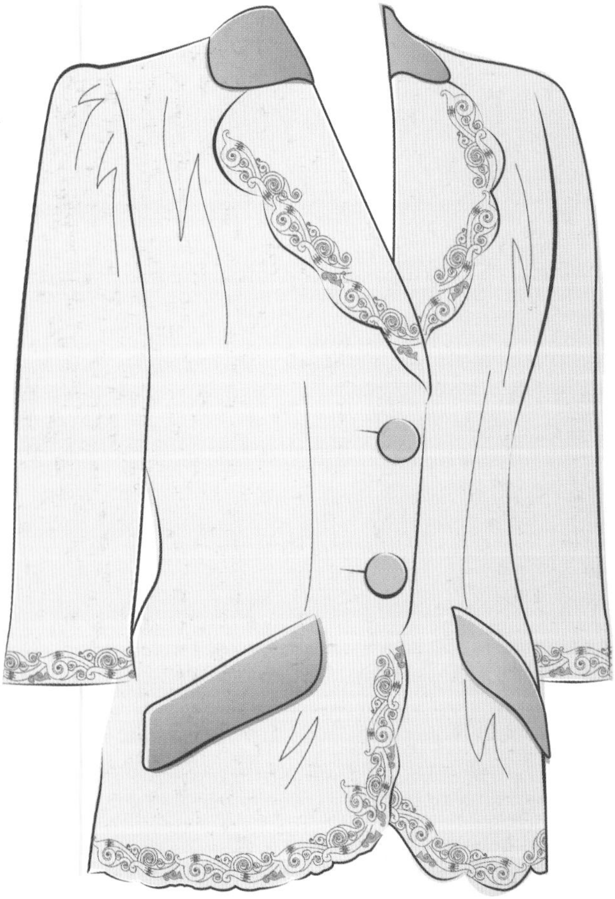

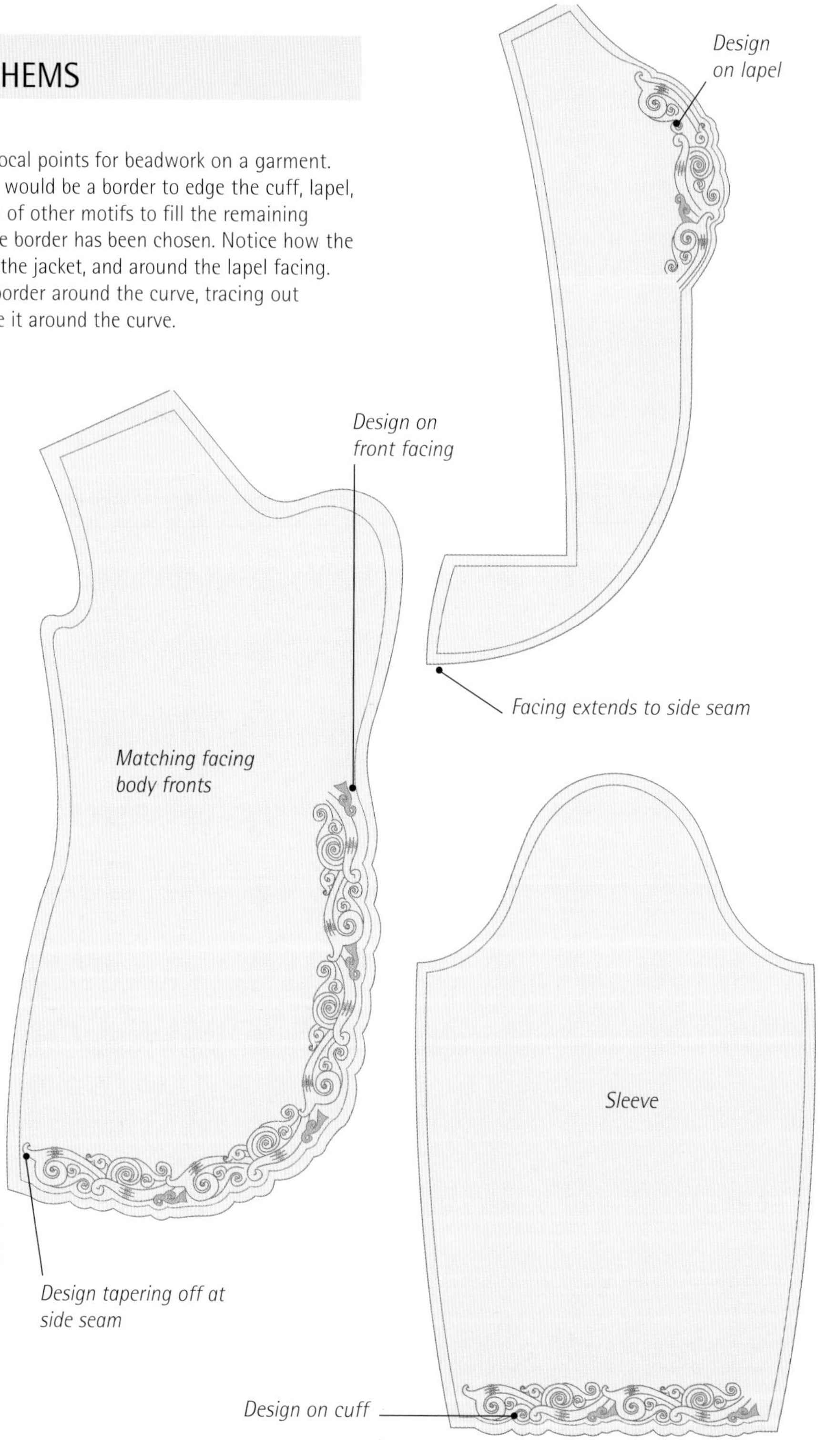

Design on lapel

Design on front facing

Matching facing body fronts

Facing extends to side seam

Sleeve

Design tapering off at side seam

Design on cuff

COMBINED PATTERNS

Ribbon Latice Border (page 71)
Baroque Lozenge (page 48)

The blending of this border with a lozenge motif shows how different designs from this book may be combined. Notice that only the lattice portion of the border is used, and, like the border used in Cuffs, Lapels, and Hems, it is traced to follow the curve of the neck line. Place the lozenge at a strategic focal point (here, the small of the back). Half the lozenge motif is used again at the neck to unite the composition.

Belt: Embroider on organza, and back with dress fabric

Back view

Baroque Lozenge placed to cover back opening

Place design centrally over any joining seams

Draft curved midline to "bend" the border around the neckline

COMBINED PATTERNS

Sapphire Bracelet (page 79)
Floral Urn (page 83)
Step and Repeat with Dangles (page 59)

This example of combined patterns shows the Sapphire Bracelet border as an edging to the neckline and jacket opening, while the body of the garment is covered with the Step and Repeat with Dangles fill. The Floral Urn motif is placed where the chest pocket would normally be. When marking the pattern, position the fill first, before adding the border and motif. Mark the fabric and stretch it into a frame. Complete the border and the motif before adding the fill.

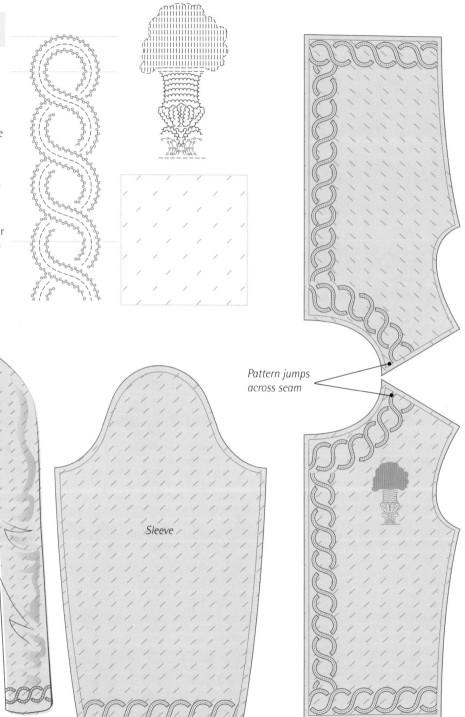

Pattern jumps across seam

Sleeve

ALL-OVER MOTIFS

Bridal Rose Vine (page 72)

The surest way to create a luxurious effect is with a heavy all-over pattern. This composition has been created using row upon row of a border, worked closely together. When planning this project, make sure the border "reads" across all dart and seam lines. The best way to do this is to make a paper model of the garment, taping all the seam lines together and any darts closed. This gives you a three-dimensional object on which to position the design. Make sure you stretch the fabric in a frame before working (see pages 30–33).

Make sure border is continuous across seam lines

Center front

Pattern jumps over fitting darts

Bend pattern to fit guide line

Plot pattern on body pieces (see blue guideline)

Pattern jumps over side seams and darts

CUFFS

Egg and Dart (page 79)

This design isn't a cuff per se, but a sleeve called the "pagoda" sleeve. It is worked in two layers, and the illustration on the right demonstrates how to draft the patterns for both layers. As you need a degree of stiffness in this piece, back the fabric with wool felt before stretching it in a frame. The Egg and Dart border is easily bent around the gentle curves on the edges.

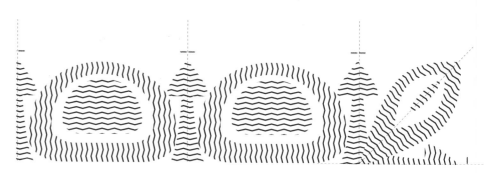

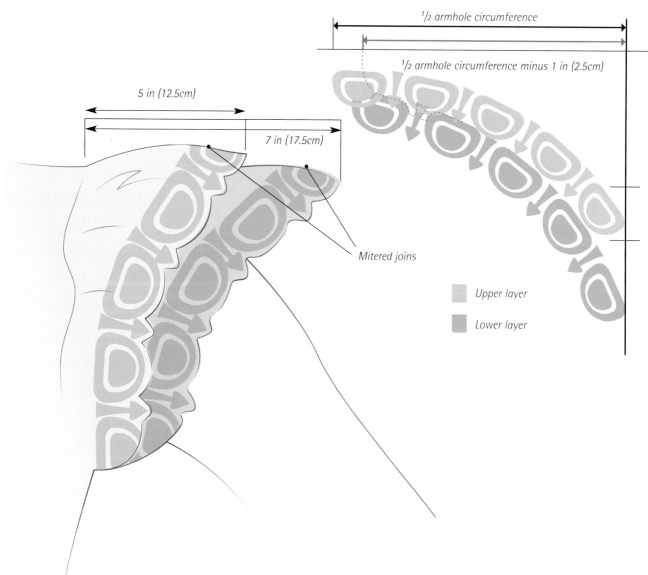

1/2 armhole circumference

1/2 armhole circumference minus 1 in (2.5cm)

5 in (12.5cm)

7 in (17.5cm)

Mitered joins

Upper layer

Lower layer

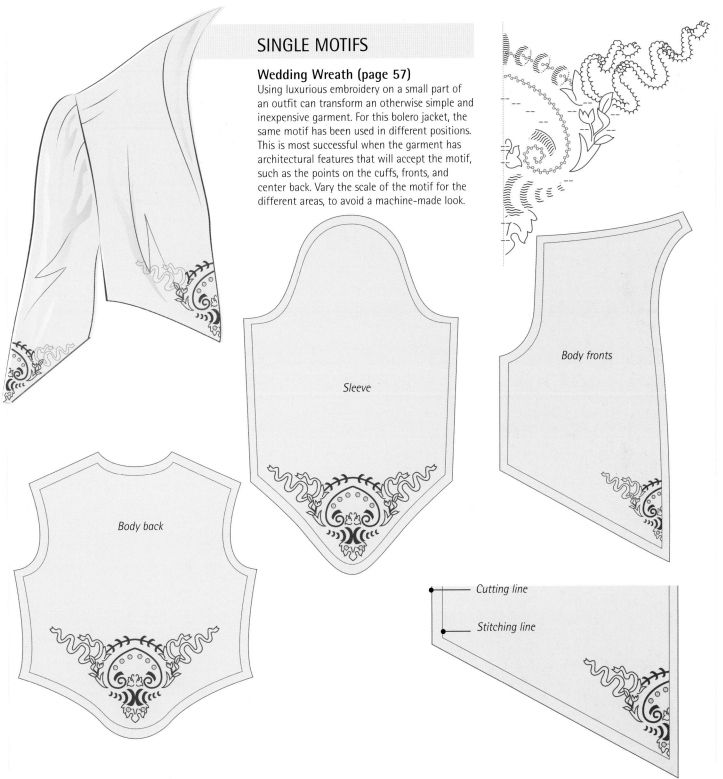

SINGLE MOTIFS

Wedding Wreath (page 57)

Using luxurious embroidery on a small part of an outfit can transform an otherwise simple and inexpensive garment. For this bolero jacket, the same motif has been used in different positions. This is most successful when the garment has architectural features that will accept the motif, such as the points on the cuffs, fronts, and center back. Vary the scale of the motif for the different areas, to avoid a machine-made look.

Sleeve

Body fronts

Body back

Cutting line

Stitching line

TRANSFERRING PATTERNS TO FABRIC

Designs can be transferred onto fabric using several methods. Use an artist's pen or chalk pencil to trace the design directly onto the fabric. A light box might be necessary for heavier fabrics. If using fabrics and beads that can be washed easily, try using water-soluble stabilizer film, or paper onto which the design has been traced. The stabilizer is tacked to the right side of the fabric, and the beading worked through it before it is washed off.

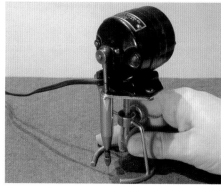

Pounce piercer

Pounce piercer

This is a small electric device that drives a needle up and down, like the action of a sewing machine. A thick pad of felt is laid on the table, with the paper on top. The needle goes through the paper into the felt pad, piercing the paper. You can get more detail and finer lines with this tool, but they are hard to find and expensive.

Pounce pad (or bag)

You can buy a pounce pad from a sign-painting supplier. It has a stopper on the top of the box, into which the pounce powder is poured. The powder sifts through the pad. Alternatively, you can make your own pounce bag using a tennis sock. Pour the pounce powder into the sock, tie a knot, and store it in a resealable bag or airtight container when not in use.

THE POUNCE METHOD

One of the most popular ways of transferring a design onto fabric is by using a pounce pattern and pounce pad. If you are familiar with quilting tools or sign-painting tools, you will know this method. A pounce pattern is a paper pattern with the design drawn onto it. The lines on the paper are then pierced with a pounce piercer or by using the empty needle on your sewing machine. The holes in the paper enable the pounce powder to sift through, marking the design lines onto the fabric.

POUNCING EQUIPMENT
Pounce powder

This is available in white, black, light blue, and pale yellow. There is a version of the white powder that vanishes with steam—this is useful in cases where you don't want the markings to show, for example, in a sparse design on the finished product. Use white for dark fabrics and vice versa. The exception is white embroidery—to eliminate the problem of a color bleeding through the finished work, you need to mark with white powder onto white fabric. It may be a little more difficult to see to work, so good light is essential.

Sizing

Use the enlarge/reduce feature on a photocopier to enlarge or reduce your design. Each of the designs in this book includes the percentage by which you should enlarge the pattern to bring it to its original size. You may also find it useful to enlarge the photographs—see page 7 for instructions.

Make several copies increasing and decreasing by 10 percent per copy. For example, enlarge by 110 percent, then 120 percent, and reduce by the same increment, 90 percent, then 80 percent. This creates a library of the motifs at different sizes that you can refer to and use later.

Pounce pad and powder

Home-made pounce pad

PREPARING A POUNCE PATTERN

Making a pounce pattern takes a little work, but the reward is that you can reuse it to duplicate the results as many times as you wish.

You will need
◎ Kraft paper
◎ Pen
◎ Light box
◎ Motif
◎ Sewing machine
◎ Iron
◎ Pounce pad or bag
◎ Pounce paper
◎ Duster
◎ Hairspray

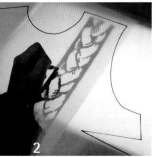

1 Draft the seam lines of the garment pattern piece onto the kraft paper and decide what your motif or combination of motifs is going to be.

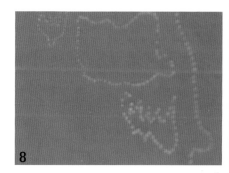

2 Determine the placement of the motifs, then transfer the motifs to the kraft paper using a light box (or a small lamp inside a box, covered with glass or Perspex).

3 Remove the bobbin case from the sewing machine, as well as the upper thread. Install a size 7 or 8 needle into the machine (a finer needle is better here).

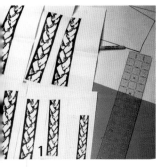

4 Drop the feed dogs (if your machine has this feature), and attach the darning foot. Move the paper under the needle and "sew" the lines you drew on the paper. This will pierce the paper to make the pounce pattern. Roll the paper section by section to navigate it through the machine.

5 When the pounce pattern is complete, press it with a dry iron to flatten out any wrinkles from the sewing machine.

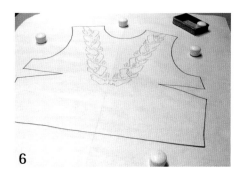

6 Place the pounce pattern on the right side of the fabric and secure with pins or weights.

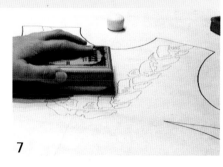

7 Rub and pat the pounce pad onto the paper, making sure you have covered the entire pattern. Before lifting the pounce pattern off the fabric, dust it with a duster misted with a little water to keep the excess dust down.

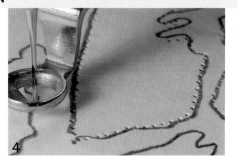

8 Gently lift off the pounce pattern to reveal the marked fabric.

Tip

If you are working with a smooth finished fabric or thin fabric, the marks may smudge or completely wipe off. To "fix" the powder, spray unscented hairspray in the air about 12 in (30cm) above the surface of the fabric. The mist that settles should be enough to fix the powder without harming the fabric. If your fabric is porous, you can skip this step. Now the fabric is ready to put into the frame.

APPLIQUÉ

One of the issues of caring for a beaded garment is cleaning it. A solution to this problem may be the use of appliqué, which involves beading onto a separate piece that is then attached to the actual garment with slipstitches. The appliqué can be removed while the garment is cleaned and then re-attached later. Another advantage to this method is the appliqué can be moved around from garment to garment. Disadvantages of appliqué work are the decrease in freedom of design—appliqué will always have a finite border—and the stiffness that appliqué imparts to the base fabric. A thin, flowing base fabric will not move as well with appliquéd pieces on it as when the beads are attached directly.

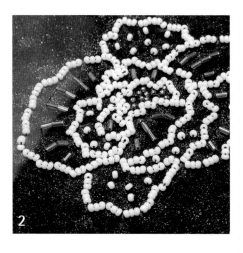

2 Embroider the appliqué design with your chosen beads.

WORKING APPLIQUÉ

This method of working appliqué describes how to avoid frayed edges and ensure the fabric finishes close to the beads. Note that white fabric glues are more flexible than epoxy glue, and easier to control than proprietary anti-fray products. Water-soluble glue is used, on the assumption that the appliqué will not be washed.

You will need
◎ Organza
◎ Design to transfer to organza
◎ Embroidery hoop
◎ Hoop frame or C-clamp
◎ Beads
◎ Thread
◎ White fabric glue
◎ Sharp embroidery scissors

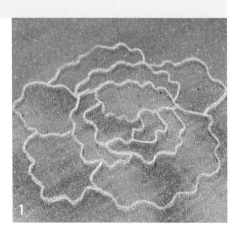

1 Place the organza in the hoop and mark your chosen design onto the fabric (see Transferring Patterns to Fabric, pages 26–27). Clamp the hoop into its frame, or onto the tabletop with a C-clamp. Set up your bead container with the beads you will use for the design.

3 When the design is completed, steam it from behind to set the stitches, and then apply glue around the edges on the back of the work. Spread the glue in a strip about 1/4 in (5mm) wide along the outer edge of the appliqué. You want to cover the outermost row of stitches. The glue will extend out past the finished edge of the appliqué.

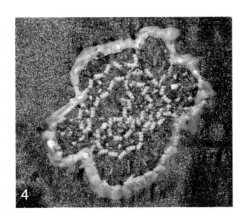

4 Keeping the work in the embroidery hoop, allow the glue to dry completely (following the manufacturer's instructions).

5 Once the glue is dry, remove the work from the hoop.

6 Use sharp embroidery scissors to cut out the appliqué. You will be cutting through the glued area. Note that the fabric doesn't fray because the glue has locked the grain in place.

7 Look at the back of the work to check how closely you can cut the fabric to the beading. Turn the work over and cut with the work right-side up, so you don't cut through sequins, or catch your scissors on the beads. Cut as close as you can without touching the stitches holding the outermost beads in place. Here, the appliqué is shown from the back, after it is cut, so you can see how the edge has been sealed.

8 Whip-stitch your finished appliqué to the garment.

USING FRAMES AND HOOPS

While thread embroidery can be worked either on fabric that is held loose or stretched taut in a frame, bead embroidery is almost always worked on fabric stretched taut in a frame. A variety of frames are available, but the types discussed here are scroll frames and embroidery hoops. If bead embroidery is worked without tension, an uneven amount of shrinkage will be introduced into the fabric, causing the fabric to shrivel and crease up. There are exceptions to this rule—see Working across a seam in Good Sewing Practice, page 33.

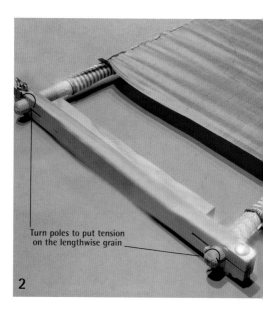

Turn poles to put tension on the lengthwise grain

2

SETTING UP A SCROLL FRAME

Setting up a frame is the essential first step to creating professional-looking beaded embroidery. It is important to get a strong, tight tension on the fabric and to ensure that the grain of the fabric is square in the frame. If the grain is not square, the embroidery will lock it "off grain," and the fabric will never hang properly.

You will need
◎ Scroll frame
◎ Needle and thread
◎ Pins
◎ Fabric with pattern marked
◎ L-square
◎ Ribbon or wide twill tape

2 Pull the fabric across to the opposite canvas carrier. Pin the opposite cross-grain edge to the carrier. Turn the poles on the frame so that you will put tension onto the lengthwise grain of the fabric, and then tighten the wing nuts. On a scroll frame, turn the opposite pole to put tension onto the fabric.

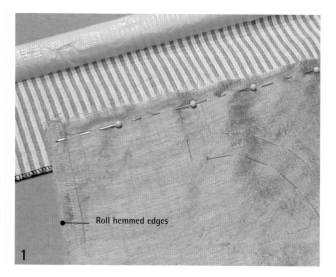

Roll hemmed edges

1

1 When you have the pattern marked on the fabric and it is ready for the frame, it is a good idea to sew a roll hem on the edges for reinforcement. On the frame, pin (or thread-baste) one cross-grain edge of the fabric to one of the canvas carriers, and tighten the wing nuts. If you are using a scroll frame, roll up any excess fabric onto one of the poles and then tighten the wing nuts.

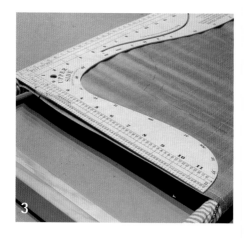

3

3 Use an L-square to make sure that the grain lines of the fabric are square. Adjust if necessary.

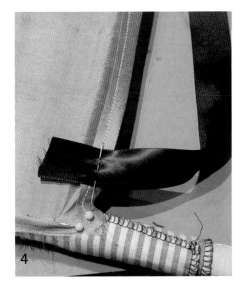

4 To create tension on the crossgrain, use ribbon or wide twill tape, and pins to attach the fabric to the frame. Starting at the bottom on the right-hand side, pin the ribbon to the roll hem on the edge of the fabric.

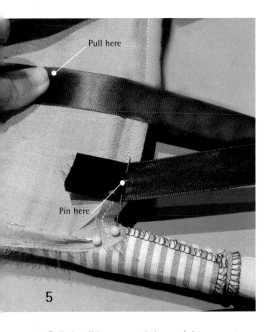

Pull here

Pin here

5 Pull the ribbon around the upright support, and back over the edge of the fabric. While holding the tension, pin the ribbon to the edge.

6 Repeat Steps 4 and 5 at the bottom edge of the left-hand side of the frame.

7 Repeat the process, working first one side and then the other, all the way up the frame.

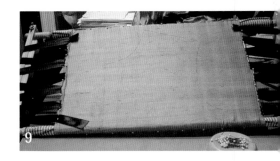

8 Work in this side-to-side pattern to keep a straight lengthwise grain with no "wobble." If you secured one edge first, then the other, the results would be uneven.

9 This is how the frame should look with the ribbons attached and the fabric mounted correctly.

10 The fabric is now under tension and ready to work.

EMBROIDERY HOOPS

Embroidery hoops are useful for small projects, such as appliqué, or for widely spaced motifs on larger pieces of fabric. Hoops come in a variety of sizes; choose a smaller one to make a project portable.

Setting up an embroidery hoop

A 12 in (30cm) diameter hoop is a good size to begin with.

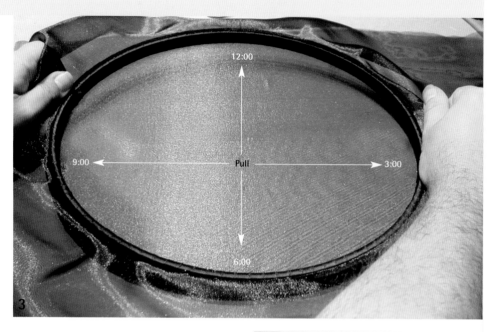

1 Hoops are made from a variety of materials, and the surface quality varies. To ensure that the hoop will not snag or damage your fabric, it is advisable to wrap both parts of it with an inexpensive ribbon.

3 Using a clock dial analogy, the straight grain runs from 12:00 to 6:00. The cross grain will be from 9:00 to 3:00. Pull the fabric tight from 12:00 to 6:00, and then from 9:00 to 3:00.

4 Pull the fabric at 10:00 and 4:00, and then at 2:00 and 8:00.

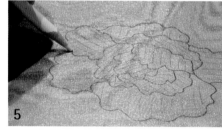

5 Once the fabric is in the hoop, you can transfer the design onto it, using either the pounce method (see pages 26–27), or an artist's colored pencil (shown here).

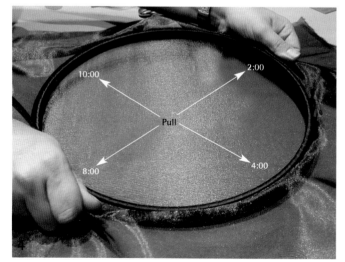

2 Lay the fabric (organza in this case) over the outer ring of the hoop and then snap the inner ring of the hoop onto the fabric. Now the fabric is caught into the hoop, ready for tension.

33

Using Frames and Hoops

GOOD SEWING PRACTICE

◎ **Environment** When you are working on a frame, ensure you have good light on the work, and use a comfortable chair that supports your back. Keep your bead containers close to hand, sitting on the surface of the fabric.

◎ **Frame height** Whether you use legs, stands, or sawhorses, the optimum height for working is chest-height. You should not have to lean into the frame to work—your back should be straight and your arms high enough to be comfortable. If you lean into the frame, it will increase fatigue and can lead to bad posture.

◎ **Order of work** Whenever possible, work the design from the middle of the frame to the outside—this keeps the tension more even.

◎ **Stab stitches** When fabric is not held taut in a frame, you can embroider using "scoop" stitches—running the needle into and out of the fabric in one motion. But with the fabric held taut for bead embroidery, you need to use what is called a "stab" stitch—push the needle through the fabric (either up or down), and completely close the stitch before starting the next. If you use a "scoop" stitch when the fabric is taut, you risk making holes in it, especially when using organza, crepe, or chiffon.

◎ **Working across a seam** If you are working on a motif that jumps across a seam, work the beading up to 1/4 in (5mm) away from the seam line, not right up to the seam line. After you sew the seam closed, work the piece in your hand (not on the frame), and fill

in the missing beads using a "scoop" stitch. You will get some shrinkage here, but it will be more even than if the fabric tension were loose.

◎ **Finishing** When you have finished the beading, steam it from behind to set the stitches, and then brush the work thoroughly to remove any powder that remains on the fabric. You can now remove the piece from the frame and check the fabric against the pattern, to correct for shrinkage. Redraft the seam lines if necessary, and add seam allowances. Now you are ready to cut out the fabric.

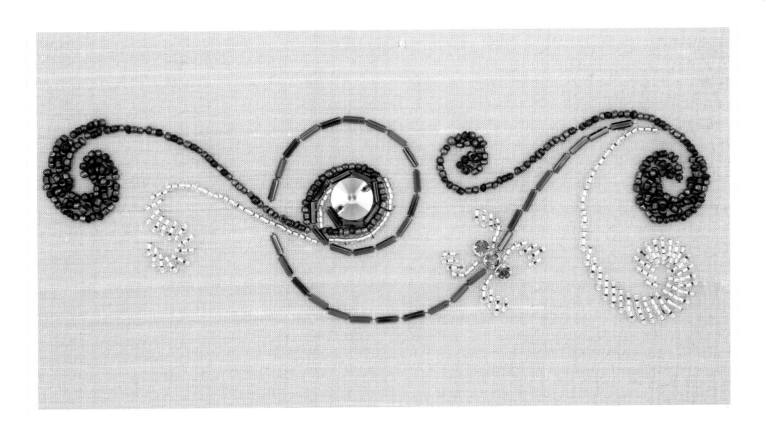

STITCH LIBRARY

In this Stitch Library, stitches are grouped into different categories, such as "backstitch" or "stop stitch," and examples of each type are shown. All of the stitches used in this book are explained here. However, if you are looking at existing pieces to gain inspiration, or if you need to duplicate or repair something, this method of categorizing stitches is extremely useful. It takes each stitch back to a basic "concept." If you understand this concept, then you can work out how similar stitches are made.

RUNNING STITCH FAMILY

Running stitch

Basic running stitch is used for stitching beads either closely in a line or widely spaced. Working from left to right, bring the needle in and out of the fabric at regular intervals, picking up the beads as you go. The stitch length should be at least as long as the bead, or slightly longer, to make the bead sit square on the fabric. Do not make the stitch shorter than the bead.

Multiple beads on a running stitch

This stitch uses a number of beads on one stitch—the number is variable to taste. The stitch length can be the same length as the total number of beads on the stitch, or it can be shorter.

A When the stitch length is the same as the total number of beads, the beads sit flat against the fabric. This is a good way to sew a line of beads quickly.

B If the stitch length is shorter than the total number of beads, the stitch will stand up from the fabric. This makes a textured line that is good for edging sections within a design.

Sequins on a running stitch

When stitching sequins using running stitch, there will be minimum thread showing, because the sequins should overlap, hiding the working thread.

1 Following a pre-drawn line, bring the thread up through the fabric, and slide the first sequin down the thread onto the fabric.
2 Insert the needle into the fabric, just to the right of the design line where it meets the edge of the sequin. Pull the stitch closed.
3 Bring the needle up from below the fabric, just to the left of the design line. Pull the stitch closed. Slide another sequin down onto the fabric.
4 Insert the needle into the fabric, just to the right of the design line where it meets the edge of the sequin. Pull the stitch closed. Repeat Steps 3 and 4 until finished.

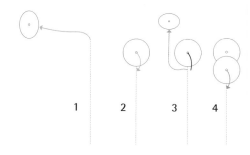

|1|2|3|4|

Sequins at an angle

Sewing sequins as described above makes the stitch length the same as the distance from the hole to the edge of the sequin. The sequin will lie flat against the fabric. If you want the sequin to incline upward from the fabric, shorten the stitch, by pushing backwards on the sequin before you insert the needle into the fabric at Step 4.

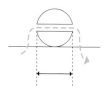

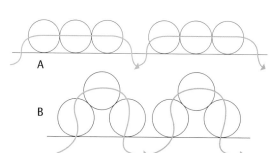

A

B

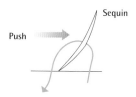

Push

Sequin

Bouclé stitch

This is a variation of multiple beads on a running stitch (see page 34). For bouclé stitch, the object is to make a long strand of beads and stitch it down with a very short stitch, so it buckles. The buckling forms a loop. The loops can be short or long, closely or sparsely spaced. Leave the thread tension a little loose. After every three to five stitches, knot off the thread without breaking it. Nymo thread is the most secure to use for this stitch.

Bouclé stitch can be used as a fill by spacing it sparsely, as a fringe if sewn in a row, or as a highly textured fill if sewn closely. The stitch remains the same but the spacing, and the number of beads on the stitch, will change the look.

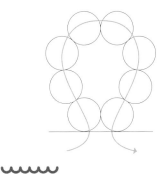

Couching stitch

The fastest (but least secure) way to sew beads in a row is with couching stitch. Knot a length of thread, bring it up through the fabric at the beginning of a line of the design, and string the desired number of beads onto it. This thread will be separate from the working thread. Lay the string of beads along the design line on the fabric. Bring the working thread up through the fabric at the same entrance point as the beaded thread, and use it to stitch the string of beads down to the fabric, stitching between the beads. It is only necessary to stitch between every third or fifth bead.

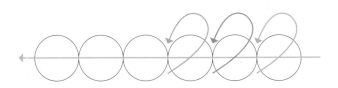

Satin stitch or zigzag stitch

This method is useful for covering large areas of a motif with beads. The direction of the bead strands in the stitches must be considered when making a design. The stitch can be flat or padded.

For the flat version, use the design lines on the fabric as your stitch guide. Thread enough beads onto a stitch to take it across the design and cover it. Use a zigzag motion to stitch back and forth across the design, increasing or decreasing the number of beads at each stitch as the pattern widens or narrows, until the area is covered. If the area is large, couch (see below left) beads down in the center if necessary.

For the padded version, cut a pad of felt, 1/16 in (2mm) smaller than the design, preferably the same color as the beads or ground fabric. Hand-tack the felt pad in place, and then work the beads over the pad. Padding is useful on napped fabrics because it keeps the beads from sinking into the nap. On flat fabrics padding provides high relief, which can give a richer finish to the work.

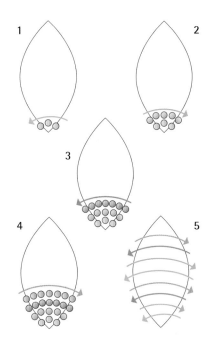

BACKSTITCH FAMILY

Basic backstitch

Backstitch is the most secure, but most time- (and thread-) consuming of stitches. It doesn't unravel easily, so it is a good choice for edging appliqués, or sewing on beads in areas where there is excessive wear. It can be sewn with one bead per stitch, or with multiple beads per stitch.

Bring the needle up and through the first bead, and down at A. Come up at B, pick up a bead, and then bring the thread back down at A. Bring the thread out ahead of B at C, pick up a bead, and bring the thread back down at B. Continue to the end.

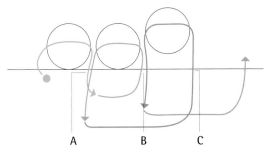

A   B   C

Large and small beads on a backstitch

This stitch is good for edging and bordering, and is flexible so it goes around curves easily. You can vary the look by changing the spacing of the large beads, or varying the relative sizes of the large and small beads.

1 The first stitch is different from the subsequent stitches. Start with a large bead, then thread on the required number of small beads, then the second large bead. Insert the needle into the fabric and close the stitch.
2, 3 & 4 For subsequent stitches, travel under the fabric and bring the needle up, using the determined spacing between the large beads. Thread on a large bead, and the same number of small beads. Then, insert the needle into the previous large bead, and close the stitch.

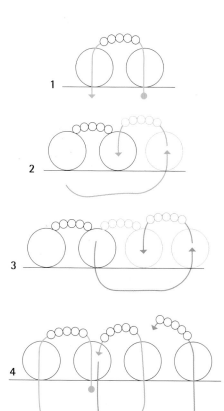

Sequins on a backstitch

Sew sequins with a backstitch for a design detail. When using backstitch, you will see a line of thread down the center of the row of sequins. You have the option of using a contrasting (or matching) embroidery thread, or of using beads on the stitch.

1 Bring the thread out on the design line. Slide one sequin down onto the fabric, and insert the needle into the fabric at the point where the line meets the edge of the sequin. Pull the stitch closed.
2 At the opposite side of the sequin, bring the needle up at the point where the line meets the edge of the sequin. Slide another sequin down onto the fabric.
3 Insert the needle into the hole of the previous sequin. Pull the stitch closed and then bring the needle up at the point where the line meets the edge of the sequin.
4 Slide another sequin down onto the fabric.
5 & 6 Repeat as many times as necessary.

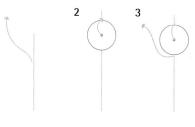
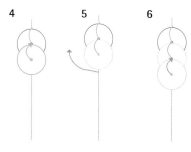

STOP STITCH FAMILY

Basic stop stitch

The stop stitch is a very useful stitch and is used frequently in beading. There are variations, but there is one important thing to remember when making any stop stitch. When inserting the needle back into a bead or beads, to close a stitch, make sure to scrape the point of the needle against the inside of the beads when passing it through. This will eliminate the possibility of stitching through the thread and creating a snarl.

1 Bring the needle up through the fabric and slide the bead of choice down onto the fabric. This bead can be any type—round, seed, bugle, or sequin. Next, pick up a seed bead, which we call the "stop" bead.
2 Insert the needle back through the bead into the fabric, and pull the stitch closed.
3 When the stitch is closed, the stop bead will sit on top of the main bead.

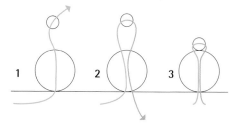

Stop stitch for flat-back gems When attaching a drilled, flat-back gem onto fabric, the classic way is to use a seed bead and thread, matching these to the color of the stone. This makes an almost invisible attachment. Attach the stone with the stop stitch as described above, but knot off after stitching each hole. This ensures that if one thread breaks you are less likely to lose a stone.

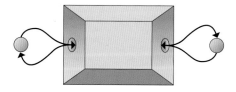

Stop stitch "two-pass"

The two-pass is a stop stitch with an additional stitch of a multiple of beads. This stitch gives the appearance that a large bead is held down onto the fabric, with the line of beads passing over the bead.

1 Make the basic stop stitch, as described above, using a large bead or flat-back gem for the main bead. The stop bead should be the same as the beads you will use for the multiple-bead stitch in Step 2.

2 Bring the needle up through the fabric, to one side of the main bead. String on a number of the small beads, to reach from the fabric to the stop bead, then pass the needle through the stop bead. On the other side of the stop bead, thread on the same number of small beads as on the other side of the stop bead.
3 Insert the needle into the fabric, on the opposite side of the bead, and close the stitch.

Two-pass stop stitch for flat-back gems

The two-pass can be used as an alternative method of sewing on flat-back gems, which makes an interesting design.

1 First, sew the gem down with a single thread stitch—match the thread to the color of the stone.
2 Using contrasting beads make a second stitch, with multiple beads, over the first stitch and into the same hole. This creates a line of beads that appear to hold the stone.

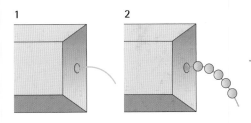

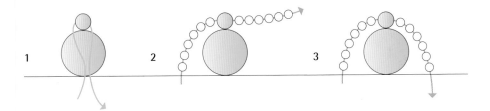

Dangle stitch

The dangle stitch is an elongated stop stitch. It can be as long or short as desired, and the combination of beads used is up to the individual. If you space the beads in a row close together, they make a fringe. The dangles give movement to a piece.

Dangle stitches are easily caught and broken, so use a strong thread such as Nymo and knot off after every one or two dangle stitches. This way, if a thread breaks, you don't create a chain reaction of unraveling. Finally, to make a dangle drape better, it is a good idea to have a heavy bead on the end.

1 Bring the needle up through the fabric and thread on the desired combination of beads to create the dangle. Then, pick up a seed bead for the stop bead.
2 Pass the needle backwards through all of the beads of the dangle, and directly into the fabric. Pull the stitch closed, using a light tension so the dangle can move freely.

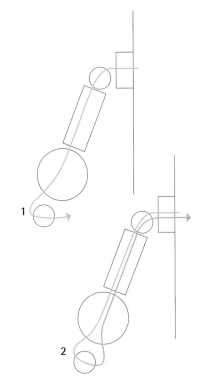

Dangle loop

The dangle loop is like a dangle stitch, but a loop of beads replaces the stop bead. You can use any number of beads to create this dangle —make samples to see what effect you like. Odd numbers work best.

1 Bring the needle up through the fabric. Thread on the desired number of beads and slide them down onto the fabric.
2 Insert the needle back through the number of beads you want for the "stem," and directly into the fabric. Pull the stitch closed.

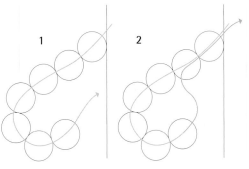

Chain stitch

The chain stitch is a series of dangle loops in a row. It makes a good border or textured line, and can be varied by the size or number of beads used. You can also vary the number of beads on each loop. Large round beads can be used to simulate clusters of grapes.

1 Make a dangle loop (see page 37). After closing it, lay it against the fabric. Bring the needle up through the fabric, inside the loop.

2 Make another dangle loop, which will be standing up (perpendicular to the fabric) inside the loop of the previous dangle loop. Lay the second loop against the fabric, and bring the needle up through the fabric, through the second loop.

3 Repeat as desired. For the last stitch in the row, couch the dangle flat against the fabric to stop the row unraveling.

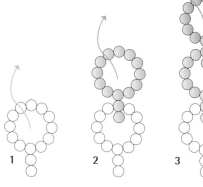

Bead mesh

Bead mesh is a valuable beading technique to master. It can be used in any number of ways: as a fill for small areas; to join two pieces of fabric; or even to create veiling (as for a hat). Bead mesh is worked "above the fabric," which means that, after the first beads are stitched into the fabric, the rest is done through the holes in the beads. The needle will not pass through the fabric at any time while making the bead mesh.

The suggested thread for bead mesh is either Silamide thread or Nymo. Use a double thread and make the working thread length very long—at least 40 in (1m). Mesh eats up thread, so the longer the thread, the more mesh you can make before knotting off and starting new thread. It is important to keep your thread tension a little loose—if you pull too tight, the mesh won't wear as well.

Bead mesh can be made from seed beads or bugle beads. Here we use bugle beads, as this makes it easier to see how the mesh takes shape. If you use seed beads, simply substitute a multiple of seed beads for one bugle bead.

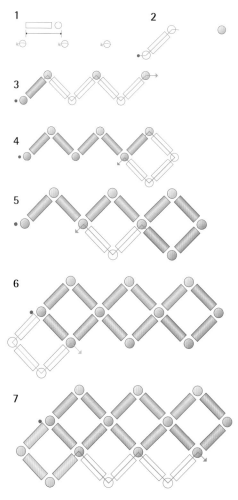

1 Decide on the width of the mesh, and then stitch down the required number of seed beads onto the fabric with a running stitch. The distance between these beads should be the minimum of the length of one bugle bead plus one seed bead. It can be a little more. Once you have sewn these beads down, knot off and cut your thread. Everything else will proceed above the fabric.

2 Begin the mesh by making a knot in the working thread, and then placing one seed bead and one bugle bead onto the thread. Pass the needle through the seed bead on the end.

3 To work across the row, thread one bugle, one seed, and one bugle bead onto the needle . Then pass the needle through the next seed bead sewn onto the fabric. Repeat across the row.

4 Turning around to start the next row uses a different stitch. Thread onto the needle one bugle, one seed, another bugle, another seed, and a third bugle bead. You will then pass the needle through the seed bead in the previous bugle-seed-bugle unit.

5 Continue along the row making the bugle-seed-bugle unit, then placing the needle through the next seed bead, as shown. Work across the row, to the end of the row.

6 Turn around to start the next row, using the same method as in Step 4. This bugle-seed-bugle-seed-bugle stitch will apply whenever you need to turn around to start a new row.

7 Repeat Steps 5 and 6 until you have the amount of mesh you desire. Knot off (see right), or add a dangle finish (see right).

Dangle finish on bead mesh

A dangle finish on bead mesh is often used on the ends of scarves and shawls. It has a nice weight and movement, and finishes such articles with sparkle. Note that making the turn to get to the next row makes the first stitch in the dangle finish different from the subsequent stitches in the row.

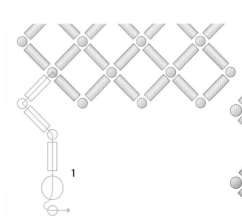

First dangle stitch

1 Once your bead mesh is the required length, start the first dangle stitch at the turn of a row. Thread on a bugle bead, a seed bead, a bugle bead, and another seed bead. Then thread on whatever your dangle will be. Pick up a stop bead on the needle.

2 Run the needle backwards through the dangle, and the last seed bead, and pull the dangle closed. Keep the thread tension a little loose. Thread on the last bugle bead, and then pass the needle through the seed bead in the bugle-seed-bugle, as shown.

Subsequent dangle stitches

1 For subsequent dangles, thread onto the needle the bugle, the seed, the dangle, and pick up the stop bead.

2 Pass the needle backwards through the dangle and the last seed bead, then pick up another bugle. Pass the needle through the seed bead in the bugle-seed-bugle, as shown. Work to the end of the row. Position to continue working the mesh.

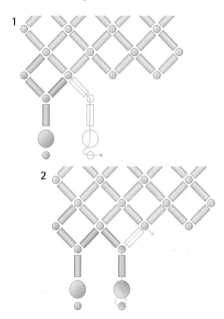

Knotting off and on in bead mesh

Don't let your working thread get shorter than 6 in (15cm) long, before you tie off. A longer thread will make tying off easier.

To knot off, pass your needle through the seed bead and then the bugle bead above it—emerging at A. Tie the thread off onto the thread at the intersection at A. Cut the thread. To add new thread, tie the new working thread onto the thread at B. Pass the needle through the bugle bead below B, and through the seed bead next to it. The thread is now in the correct position to continue working the mesh.

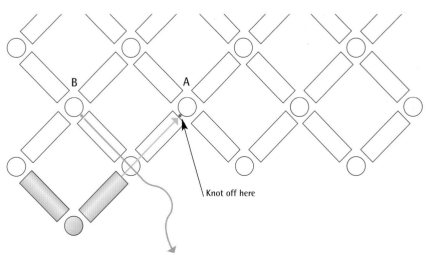

Knot off here

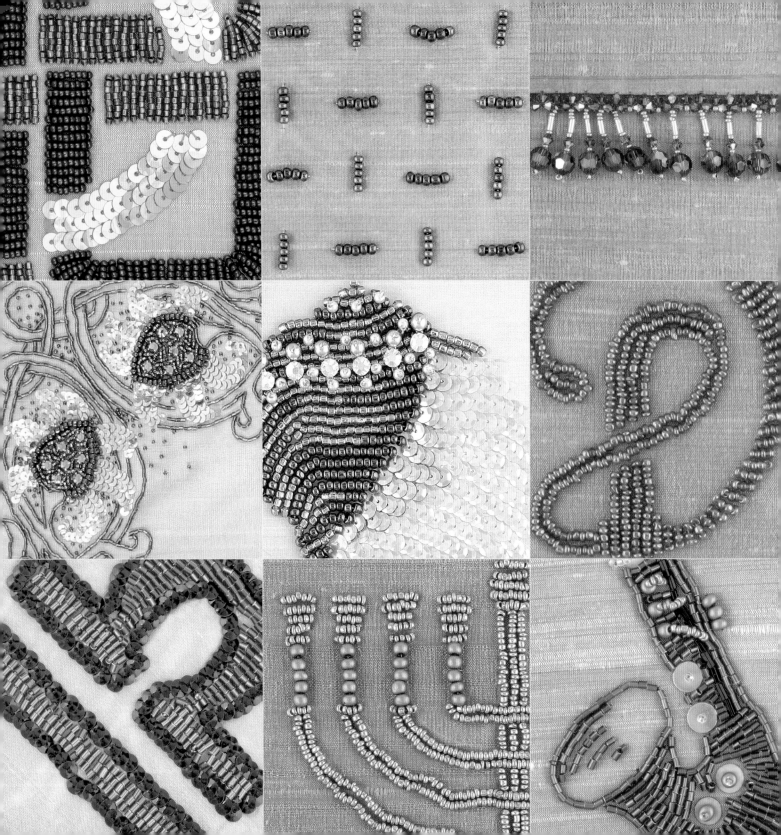

CHAPTER 2
DESIGNS

The designs shown in this section have been grouped into different categories for ease of use: Architectural Ornament; Fills; Edges; Borders; Flowers, Shells, and Insects; an alphabet for personalizing items; a zodiac for the astrologically attuned; holiday motifs for annual celebrations; and music motifs for the musically inclined. Feel free to pick and choose from the different categories to create unique compositions that reflect your own personal style. Each design features a photograph, a pattern illustration that may be enlarged, a list of the stitches and beads required, and full instructions for completing each design.

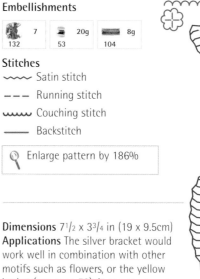

WANDS AND SPEARS

SILVER BRACKET

Embellishments

5	7	5	40
165	149	161	131

10g	6g	10g
52	76	9

Stitches

〜〜〜 Satin stitch

--- Running stitch

o–o–o Sequins on a running stitch

wwww Couching stitch

ᵒ⋅ᵒ⋅ᵒ Multiple beads on a stitch

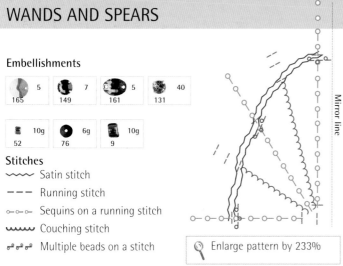

Mirror line

🔍 Enlarge pattern by 233%

Embellishments

7	20g	8g
132	53	104

Stitches

〜〜〜 Satin stitch

--- Running stitch

wwww Couching stitch

——— Backstitch

🔍 Enlarge pattern by 186%

Dimensions 6¼ x 5½ in (16 x 14cm)
Applications The wands and spears ornament is a versatile motif that can be used to support another motif or as a complete oval, by mirror-imaging it. As an oval, it would be a beautiful accent to a luxurious throw pillow.
Method Sew the 12mm stones, the 10 x 7 stones, the 8mm roses montées, and 4 of the chaton montées into position with running stitch. Next, create the "wands": Thread on alternating chaton montées and 6/0 iridescent gold seed beads until you bridge the gap between the hub of the motif and the 8mm roses montées, and then couch these down to the design line. Sew the sequins cup-down starting from the hub, using sequins on a running stitch. At the side of each of the 10 x 7 stones, sew on 7 of the 11/0 gold seed beads using multiple beads on a stitch. Finally, fill in the oval with 11/0 seed beads in satin stitch using 5 beads per stitch. Sew on an angle so that it looks like twisted rope when done.

Dimensions 7½ x 3¾ in (19 x 9.5cm)
Applications The silver bracket would work well in combination with other motifs such as flowers, or the yellow basket (see page 50). It can serve as a pedestal to set off another ornament. Use it on the center back of a kimono-style jacket or on the corners of an evening shawl.
Method Sew on the chaton montées with running stitch and then couch-stitch 5mm silver bugle beads onto the top of the motif. Fill in the areas indicated for satin stitch with the 11/0 silver seed beads, and also sew them onto the outlines using multiple beads on a backstitch—3 beads per stitch. Finally, sew on the rest of the 5mm silver bugle beads with running stitch.

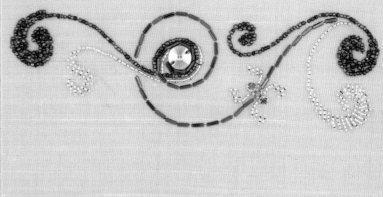

BAROQUE WINDOW

SPRING SCROLLS

Embellishments

	6		6g		2g		8g
161		72		73		51	

	4g		6g		8g
9		96		104	

Stitches

〜〜〜 Couching stitch

--- Running stitch

o–o–o Sequins on a running stitch

🔍 Enlarge pattern by 185%

Embellishments

	1		3		6g
166		130		108	

	10g		10g
53		37	

Stitches

〜〜 Satin stitch

--- Running stitch

—— Backstitch

〜〜〜 Bouclé stitch

🔍 Enlarge pattern by 194%

Mirror line

Dimensions 6¹/₂ x 4¹/₂ in (16.5 x 11cm)
Applications The baroque window is an elaborate motif that would work well on a period costume or other items where you want to evoke the eighteenth century. This motif works well vertically or horizontally.
Method Sew on the 10 x 7 stones with running stitch. Use sequins on a running stitch, first for the matte gold sequins, and then to surround the flat-back stones at top and bottom with bright gold sequins. Sew 6/0 seed beads onto the top and bottom motifs as marked using running stitch, and then couch-stitch them to surround the two stones at the sides of the motif. Couch-stitch the 2mm gold bugle beads and the 11/0 seed beads onto the lines as marked. Finally, make the "windowpanes" by couch-stitching the 5mm silver bugle beads.

Dimensions 7¹/₂ x 2¹/₄ in (19 x 6cm)
Applications Decorate the sides of a V-neckline with mirror images of this delicate motif. It is simple to execute and yet it provides a lovely grace to any neckline.
Method Sew on the 12mm stone and the 3 4mm chaton montées with running stitch, and then the bugle beads with backstitch. Sew on the 11/0 silver seed beads with multiple beads on a backstitch (3 beads per stitch) to fill in the lines reserved for them. At the ends of the lines fill the scrolls with silver seed beads in satin stitch. Outline the upper scrolls with iridescent blue seed beads using multiple beads on a backstitch (2 beads per stitch), then fill in the space inside using the same beads and bouclé stitch—5 beads per stitch.

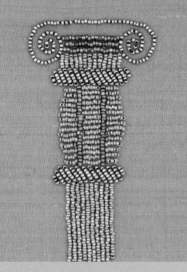

CORINTHIAN COLUMN

DECO SCROLLS

Embellishments

10g 57	7g 56	10g 31

Stitches

wwww Couching stitch

∼∼∼ Satin stitch

——— Backstitch

🔍 Enlarge pattern by 133%

Dimensions 4¹/₂ x 2¹/₄ in (11 x 6cm)

Applications When a small motif for trimming a lapel is called for, use the Corinthian column—its small size and easy execution make it a good choice for livening up a sober outfit.

Method Couch-stitch pearlescent gray seed beads to create the column, then make the horizontal bands of the capital with sage green seed beads in satin stitch. Use the same beads with multiple beads on a backstitch (2 beads per stitch) to outline the scroll at the top of the capital. Fill in the horizontal lines below the scroll and the vertical dividing lines below that with couch-stitched iridescent gray seed beads. Finally, satin-stitch pearlescent gray seed beads to fill in the remaining areas on the capital.

Embellishments

8 129	2 132	10g 33	5g 48
7g 40	15g 58	5g 79	5g 73

Stitches

wwww Couching stitch

∼∼∼ Satin stitch

——— Backstitch

- - - Running stitch

o–o–o Sequins on a running stitch

🖉🖉🖉 Multiple beads on a stitch

10g 23

🔍 Enlarge pattern by 292%

Dimensions 7 x 5¹/₂ in (17.5 x 14cm)

Applications This art deco ornament evokes the glamor of old Hollywood movies. Embroider it on a pocket or handbag to make a dramatic accent for a vintage-inspired evening outfit.

Method Sew the 4mm and 8mm chaton montées into position with running stitch, and then outline the different scrolls with multiple beads on a backstitch: first the yellow beads, then the turquoise beads to outline the turquoise scroll and the five "speed" lines. Satin-stitch the dark purple seed beads in the area indicated and then sew on the poison green sequins using sequins on a running stitch working from the end of the scroll toward the chaton monté. Sew on the 4mm gold flat sequins, again working from the end of the scroll, then fill in the central scroll with the red-orange beads—first outline the scroll with the couching stitch, and then use multiple beads on a stitch to fill in the scroll. Finally, satin-stitch the gunmetal gray beads as indicated in the diagram, running the stitches vertically.

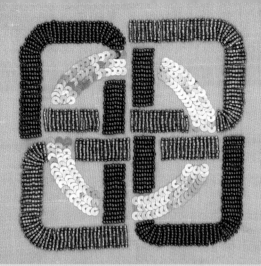

ROUND CELTIC KNOT

SQUARE CELTIC KNOT

Embellishments

	4		10g		10g
133		51		78	

Stitches

〜〜〜 Satin stitch

--- Running stitch

o-o-o Sequins on a running stitch

🔍 Enlarge pattern by 228%

Embellishments

	7g		20g		20g
73		49		52	

Stitches

〜〜〜 Satin stitch

o-o-o Sequins on a running stitch

🔍 Enlarge pattern by 260%

Dimensions 5¹/₄ x 5 in (13 x 12cm)

Applications This is one of a pair of Celtic knots drawn from a building in New York City. It works with a variety of decorative styles, from art nouveau, to art deco, to oriental. Place this at the nape of the neck on a jacket.

Method First, sew on the 5mm flat sequins with sequins on a running stitch. Begin with the central row in each section, working from the center to the outside, and then stitch on the other two rows in the same direction. Make sure the rows overlap slightly for good coverage. Next, sew on the 4 chaton montées with running stitch, and then fill in the circle surrounding the motif with gold seed beads in satin stitch—3 beads per stitch. Stitch on a diagonal to achieve the effect of twisted rope.

Dimensions 5¹/₄ x 5¹/₄ in (13 x 13cm)

Applications This is the second of the pair of Celtic knots from a building in New York City. Like its companion (left), it works with a variety of decorative styles. The square shape of this ornament makes it perfect for pockets or a small evening bag.

Method Sew on the sequins with sequins on a running stitch. Sew the middle row first in either direction, then sew the two outside rows in the same direction—make sure the sequins overlap slightly for good coverage. Next, fill in the areas denoted for satin stitch with the iridescent gold and copper seed beads as shown in the photograph. Use 8 beads per stitch to get a consistent width throughout the piece.

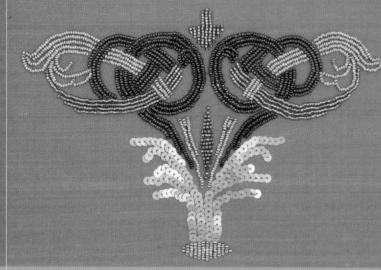

LAUREL WREATH

FOUNTAIN

Embellishments

48	20g

Stitches

⌒⌒⌒ Multiple beads on a stitch

〜〜 Satin stitch

🔍 Enlarge pattern by 175%

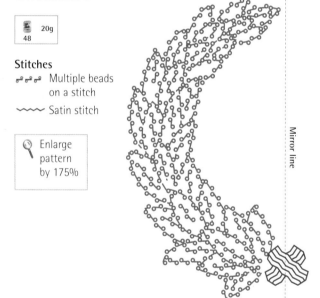

Mirror line

Dimensions 6¹/₄ x 5¹/₂ in (16 x 14cm)
Applications The laurel wreath is symbolic of honor and achievement. Use this wreath on articles that commemorate an achievement of a loved one, such as wall hangings and scrapbook covers.
Method This motif looks very rich but it is easy to work. The leaves are all outlined with the 11/0 yellow seed beads, using multiple beads on a stitch— 3 beads per stitch. After outlining the leaves, fill in the knot at the center bottom with the same 11/0 seed beads in satin stitch.

Embellishments

52 15g	51 15g	40 15g	73 5g	72 5g	49 12g

Stitches

〜〜〜 Couching stitch

○—○—○ Sequins on a running stitch

〜〜 Satin stitch

🔍 Enlarge pattern by 163%

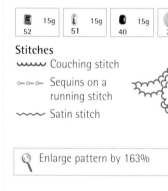

Mirror line

Dimensions 8¹/₄ x 5¹/₂ in (21 x 14cm)
Applications This motif is inspired by the Wallace Fountains in Paris. Its graceful lines would work well on the corners of an evening shawl, or would be a luxurious finish to elaborate table runners for your most festive dinners.
Method Couch-stitch the iridescent gold, bright gold, copper, and dark purple seed beads onto the fabric in the rows denoted on the diagram. Next, satin-stitch the areas indicated in the diagram with the iridescent gold seed beads and the bright gold seed beads. Note the direction of the stitches in the diagram. Finally, make the "water" in the fountain by sewing on the bright gold and matte gold sequins with sequins on a running stitch.

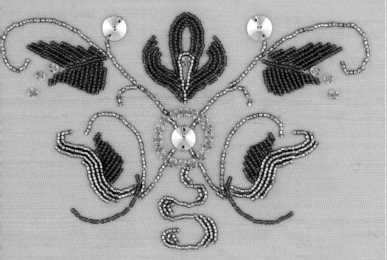

VINES AND FLOWERS

DELICATE SCROLLS

Embellishments

⬤ 166	3	✳ 130	30	▪ 39	15g	▪ 41	15g	

Stitches

〰 Couching stitch

- - - Running stitch

∿ Satin stitch

— Backstitch

🔍 Enlarge pattern by 192%

Embellishments

⬤ 164	3	◐ 149	5	▪ 49	10g	▪ 28	15g	⬤ 81	5g	⬤ 62	4g

Stitches

〰 Couching stitch

- - - Running stitch

— Backstitch

∿ Bouclé stitch

∘–∘–∘ Sequins on a running stitch

🔍 Enlarge pattern by 185%

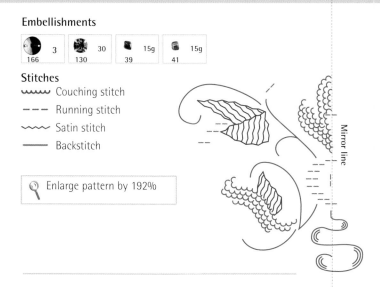

Mirror line

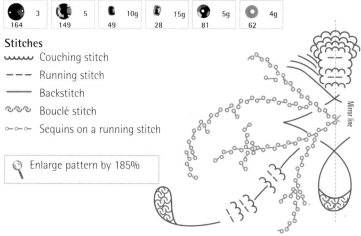

Mirror line

Dimensions 7 x 4³/₄ in (18 x 11.5cm)

Applications In the late nineteenth century, delicate motifs such as this one adorned all manner of objects. This motif would be appropriate wherever an abstract but traditional ornament is called for—either home furnishings or evening clothes.

Method Sew on the 12mm stones and the 4mm chaton montées with running stitch and then use multiple beads on a backstitch—3 beads per stitch—to trace the vine lines in the design using the iridescent purple seed beads and purple-blue seed beads. Fill the petal on the lower blossoms and the top blossom around the rose monté with couch-stitched iridescent purple seed beads. Fill the upper petal in the lower blossoms, as well as the upper blossoms, with purple-blue seed beads in satin stitch. Finally, couch-stitch purple-blue seed beads to fill the top.

Dimensions 7¹/₂ x 4 in (19 x 10cm)

Applications This companion motif mixes well with Vines and Flowers (see left), when executed in the same color combination. It also works well on its own where a delicate abstract motif is required.

Method Sew on the 12mm stones and the 8mm roses montées with running stitch. Sew down the iridescent light green seed beads using multiple beads on a backstitch—3 beads per stitch, and then couch-stitch the copper seed beads into position. Using the same beads and bouclé stitch, fill in the tips of the bottom tendrils—use 5 beads per stitch, closely packed. Use sequins on a running stitch to sew on the lines of 4mm copper cup sequins cup down—work from the outside toward the center, and then do the same for the lines of 3mm pearl beige flat sequins.

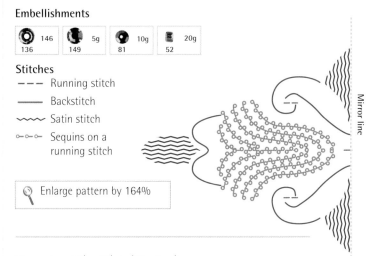

BAROQUE LOZENGE

ABSTRACT ROSETTE

Embellishments

130 : 8	166 : 2	40 : 20g
53 : 10g	41 : 10g	104 : 10g

Stitches
- - - Running stitch
~~~ Couching stitch
~~ Satin stitch

Embellishments

136 : 146	149 : 5g	81 : 10g	52 : 20g

Stitches
- - - Running stitch
—— Backstitch
~~ Satin stitch
o—o—o Sequins on a running stitch

Enlarge pattern by 164%

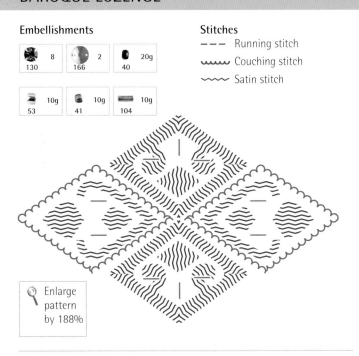

Enlarge pattern by 188%

Dimensions 7¹/₂ x 3¹/₂ in (19 x 9cm)

Applications This rosette will work horizontally or vertically, alone or spaced over a large area such as a skirt or table covering.

Method Sew on the 5 8mm roses montées with running stitch and then fill in the areas reserved for sequins using sequins on a running stitch—sew these cup-down and begin the rows at the center base of the flower and work to the tips. Sew the iridescent gold seed beads in place using satin stitch and sew the 3mm lochrosen onto the line with backstitch as described below.

Step 1 Thread on one lochrosen, and stitch backwards to secure.

Step 2 Bring the needle up on the design line, the distance of half a lochrosen.

Step 3 Thread on another lochrosen.

Step 4 Insert the needle into the previous lochrosen—close the stitch.

Step 5 Again on the design line, bring the needle up the distance of half a lochrosen.

Step 6 Thread on another lochrosen.

Step 7 Insert the needle into the previous lochrosen. Repeat these steps until the lines are covered.

Dimensions 6³/₄ x 4¹/₄ in (17 x 10.5cm)

Applications This would make a beautiful ornament for the flap of an evening bag or a lovely trim for the tops of pockets. If laid end to end, it could make a luxurious border for an evening shawl.

Method Sew on the 4mm chaton montées with running stitch and then fill in the central four diamond shapes with the silver seed beads in satin stitch. Fill the area reserved for the iridescent purple seed beads with satin stitch and couch-stitch the silver bugle beads on the outline as marked. Satin-stitch the remaining areas with dark purple seed beads as shown in the photograph and, for the finishing touch, sew the 12mm tanzanite stones to the motif with running stitch.

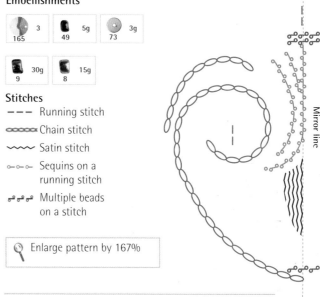

PINK DIADEM

ABSTRACT OWL

Embellishments

22	3	72	7g	5g	4g
129	132	134	88	51	53

Stitches

- - - - Running stitch

——— Backstitch

〜〜〜 Satin stitch

○–○–○ Sequins on a running stitch

〰〰〰 Couching stitch

🔍 Enlarge pattern by 170%

Dimensions 6¹/₂ x 2¹/₂ in (16.5 x 6.5cm)

Applications This feminine motif is a delight. Positioned right side up or upside down, it will beautify a neckline, top of pockets, or the flap of an evening bag.

Method Sew the 3 8mm chaton montées and all the 4mm chaton montées into position with running stitch. Satin-stitch the gold seed beads in the areas indicated on the diagram. Next, couch-stitch gold and silver seed beads to finish the top point of the diadem. Sew the first row of sequins cup-down, and the second row cup-up using sequins on a running stitch. Finally, sew the 3mm lochrosen in place using backstitch (see Abstract Rosette, page 48, for instructions).

Embellishments

3	5g	3g
165	49	73

30g	15g
9	8

Stitches

- - - - Running stitch

∞∞∞∞ Chain stitch

〜〜〜 Satin stitch

○–○–○ Sequins on a running stitch

⌐◟◞⌐ Multiple beads on a stitch

🔍 Enlarge pattern by 167%

Dimensions 5¹/₄ x 5 in (13 x 12cm)

Applications This heart-shaped motif resembles the face of an owl. It would look well as an ornament for a handbag of this shape or as the finish on the point of a deep V-neckline on the back of an evening gown.

Method Sew on the 3 12mm stones using running stitch and then fill in the area reserved for the copper seed beads with satin stitch. Next, sew on the sequins using sequins on a running stitch—work the lines bottom to top. Chain-stitch the 6/0 iridescent gold seed beads using 11 beads per stitch and 1 bead per stem. Start at the stone and work outward, ending (and both lines meeting) at the bottom center. Work the line reserved for the 6/0 gold seed beads in the same direction. To finish, use the iridescent gold beads with multiple beads (5) on a stitch to join the two rows of chain stitch at the center bottom. At the top, beneath the flat-back stone, make two stitches, the first with 5 beads, the one below it with 3 beads.

CELTIC LOZENGE

Embellishments

▨ 20g	▨ 20g	▨ 20g	▨ 20g
52	29	32	49

Stitches

∞∞∞∞ Chain stitch

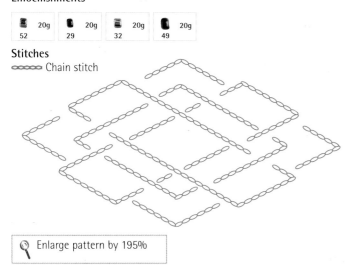

🔍 Enlarge pattern by 195%

Dimensions 6³/₄ x 3³/₄ in (17 x 9.5cm)

Applications This lozenge motif is simple but dramatic. It would make a beautiful embellishment for the chest pocket on a jacket or, turned horizontally, a striking ornament for a handbag.

Method Work this entire motif in chain stitch. The units consist of 13 seed beads and the "stem" of the loops is 2 beads. You can work the lines in any direction you wish—the texture will look the same.

YELLOW BASKET

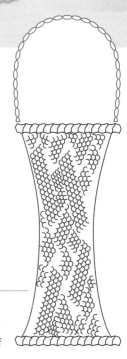

Embellishments

▨ 30g
48

Stitches

∞∞∞∞ Chain stitch

――― Backstitch

wwww Couching stitch

~~~~ Satin stitch

🔍 Enlarge pattern by 256%

Dimensions 8³/₄ x 3¹/₄ in (22.5 x 8cm)

Applications The basket is a familiar motif in architecture—it is used on the facades of buildings or as the finishing touch at the tops of pillars and towers. This whimsical version in canary yellow is in homage to Ella Fitzgerald and her song.

Method Begin by outlining the basket sides using multiple beads on a backstitch—3 beads per stitch. Next, couch-stitch the woven portions of the basket. Couch the beads in the directions indicated in the diagram to create the woven effect. Finish the top edge and the base of the basket in satin stitch. Finally, use chain stitch to create the handle—start at the top edge of the basket and work toward the center top. The loops have 15 beads and no stem.

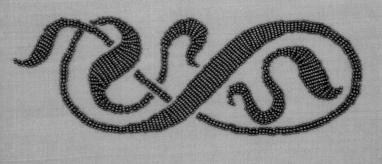

NOUVEAU SCROLL

SCROLL AND POPPY

Embellishments

50g
29

Stitches

〰〰 Satin stitch

🔍 Enlarge pattern by 240%

Dimensions 9 x 2³/₄ in (23 x 7cm)

Applications The nouveau scroll is an abstract ornament that works well both vertically and horizontally. It would make a fine embellishment around a deep cuff for a dressing gown or, scaled down, a beautiful trim for the top edge of pockets.

Method The entire motif is composed of satin stitch using the 11/0 iridescent dark green seed beads. It is important to follow the directions of the stitching on the diagram.

Embellishments

30g
52

20g
40

20
135

Stitches

〰〰 Satin stitch

——— Backstitch

- - - Running stitch

🔍 Enlarge pattern by 272%

Dimensions 9³/₄ x 2¹/₄ in (24.5 x 5.5cm)

Applications The scroll and poppy is a companion ornament to the nouveau scroll (see left). It would look wonderful as the lapel motif on a jacket or placed end to end horizontally as a border. The two ornaments in combination have many uses.

Method Outline the flowers and stems with the iridescent gold seed beads using multiple beads on a backstitch—2 beads per stitch. Satin-stitch the same beads in the areas indicated on the diagram, and then satin-stitch the dark purple seed beads to fill the centers of the flowers and other areas indicated. Finally, sew the 3mm lochrosen in place with running stitch.

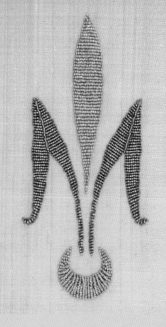

GRYPHON

Embellishments

30g 49	30g 52	11 131	1 129
10g 72	10g 73	5g 106	3g 86

Stitches

 Satin stitch

– – – Running stitch

—— Backstitch

o–o–o Sequins on a running stitch

🔍 Enlarge pattern by 479%

Dimensions 9 x 7½ in (23 x 19cm)

Applications This gryphon was inspired by the fantastical creatures carved into the cathedrals of Europe. It would look wonderful as a wall hanging.

Method Sew on the copper seed beads using multiple beads on a backstitch—3 beads per stitch. Next, fill in the areas indicated with the same seed beads in satin stitch. Sew the 11/0 iridescent gold seed beads into place with multiple beads on a backstitch and fill in the areas denoted on the diagram with the same beads in satin stitch. Attach the 4mm chaton montées using the running stitch and fill in the lines on the wing with 4mm matte gold sequins. Sew the mane in 4mm bright gold sequins, starting at the base of the wings and working toward the head—work each line of the mane from the stone outward. Finish the mane with a line of 6mm bugle beads spaced close together using running stitch. Finally, make the gryphon's beard with translucent off-white cup sequins, working from the ends of the beard toward the head.

ARROWHEAD

Embellishments

40g 51	40g 52

Stitches

  Satin stitch

🔍 Enlarge pattern by 217%

Dimensions 8¾ x 4 in (22 x 10cm)

Applications This abstract arrowhead design lends itself to many different applications. It works well when mixed with gothic motifs or modern themes and can be scaled up or down easily.

Method Work this motif entirely in satin stitch. For the most even-textured result, start in the center of each section of the motif and work the satin stitch outward. Be sure to follow the directions of the stitching in the diagram.

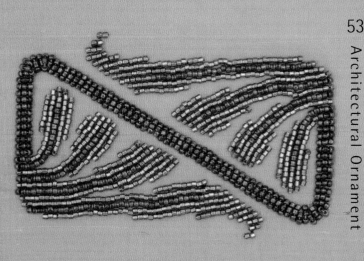

SCROLL AND DART

ACANTHUS

Embellishments

41	20g	40	30g	51	15g
166	3	132	4	128	8

Stitches

〜〜 Satin stitch

—— Backstitch

--- Running stitch

🔍 Enlarge pattern by 231%

Mirror line

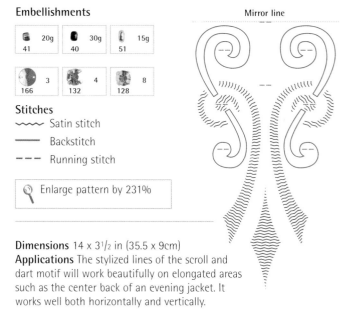

Dimensions 14 x 3¹/₂ in (35.5 x 9cm)

Applications The stylized lines of the scroll and dart motif will work beautifully on elongated areas such as the center back of an evening jacket. It works well both horizontally and vertically.

Method Sew the 4mm and 8mm chaton montées in place with running stitch, then sew on the 12mm flat-back stones using the methods outlined on page 37. Outline the scrolls with gold seed beads using multiple beads on a backstitch—3 beads per stitch. Next, fill in the point of the dart with satin-stitched iridescent purple seed beads. Work from the center of the motif to the ends. Finally, finish the sides of the dart using dark purple seed beads in satin stitch to fill in the motif. Work from the points of the section to the scrolls, ending at the chaton montées. Follow the stitch direction shown in the diagram.

Embellishments

5	30g	3	30g

Stitches

〜〜 Satin stitch

wwww Couching stitch

🔍 Enlarge pattern by 235%

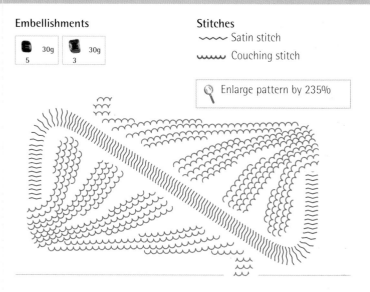

Dimensions 7¹/₂ x 5 in (19 x 12cm)

Applications This rendition of the acanthus pattern from ancient Greek architecture would be an effective motif to cover an entire evening handbag. You can work it vertically or horizontally and put it side by side with its mirror image to make pockets or handbags.

Method This is a relatively simple motif to execute. Begin by using the iridescent dark blue beads in satin stitch to fill the Z-shaped portion of the motif. The rest of the design is couching stitch, with the rows worked next to each other. String the beads so that there is a vein of iridescent dark blue beads in the leaves, while the rest are iridescent aquamarine beads.

Embellishments

30g 29	30g 49	10g 96	5g 73	5g 81	1 132	1 166
2 161	20 129	6 106	4 145	2 147	2 112	2 141

Stitches

〰️ Satin stitch

— Backstitch

- - - Running stitch

⌇ Couching stitch

∘–∘–∘– Sequins on a running stitch

Enlarge pattern by 222%

COMEDY MASK

Dimensions 8 x 4¹/₂ in (20 x 11cm)

Applications The comedy mask and its companion, the tragedy mask (see page 55), are a familiar sight in theaters and opera houses. These two masks would make a worthy ornament to the pockets of an evening wrap or coat designed to be worn out to the theater.

Method Sew the 8mm chaton monté and 8 of the 10 4mm chaton montées to the headband of the diadem using running stitch. Couch-stitch 2mm gold bugle beads to outline the headband of the diadem, and then sew the 12mm flat-back stone, the two 10 x 7 stones, and the two remaining 4mm chaton montées in place with running stitch.

Next, satin-stitch the copper seed beads to fill in the hair over the diadem. Use the iridescent dark green seed beads with multiple beads on a backstitch (3 beads per stitch) to outline the eyes, nose, and chin, and then use the same beads to fill in the mouth with satin stitch. Create the eyelashes with 6mm bugle beads using running stitch. Next, sew on the 4mm flat sequins with sequins on a running stitch to fill in the ovals on either side of the mask. Outline the lower part of the headdress with copper seed beads using multiple beads on a backstitch—3 beads per stitch.

For the tassels, start with the copper seed beads in satin stitch and then create the strands of the tassel with the 4mm cup sequins sewn cup-down. Finally, connect the tassels to the headdress with a long couching stitch. On this stitch is a copper seed bead, then 1 6mm faceted bead, 1 4mm faceted bead, 1 22mm bugle bead, 1 8mm faceted bead, and 1 6mm faceted bead, each separated by a copper seed bead. Couch this thread down to complete the headdress.

Embellishments

▪ 30g 58	▮ 30g 56	▬ 10g 97	● 5g 83	● 5g 76	● 1 164	⬭ 2 162
✳ 11 130	⬡ 2 144	⬢ 2 139	⬣ 2 146	╱ 2 113		

Stitches

〜〜〜 Satin stitch

——— Backstitch

– – – Running stitch

wwww Couching stitch

○–○–○ Sequins on a running stitch

TRAGEDY MASK

Dimensions 8 x 4½ in (20 x 11cm)

Applications The tragedy mask with its companion, the comedy mask (see page 54), completes the pair of this classic motif.

Method Sew on 9 of the 11 4mm chaton montées to the headband of the diadem using running stitch, and then outline the headband with couch-stitched 2mm bugle beads. Next, sew in place the 12mm stone, the 2 10 x 7 stones, and the 2 remaining 4mm chaton montées with running stitch.

Satin-stitch gunmetal gray seed beads to fill in the hair over the diadem and then use iridescent gray seed beads and multiple beads on a backstitch (3 beads per stitch) to outline the eyes, nose, and chin. Use the same beads to fill in the mouth with satin stitch. Fill in the ovals on either side of the mask with 6mm silver flat sequins and sequins on a running stitch. Outline the lower part of the headdress with gunmetal gray seed beads and multiple beads on a backstitch (3 beads per stitch).

Create the top of the tassels with satin-stitched gunmetal gray seed beads, and make the strands of the tassel with 4mm cup sequins sewn cup-down. Finally, connect the tassels to the headdress by making a long couching stitch. On this stitch is 1 iridescent gray seed bead, followed by 1 4mm AB faceted bead, 1 iridescent gray seed bead, 1 4mm black faceted bead, 1 29mm bugle bead, 1 more seed bead, and 1 6mm faceted bead. String these beads onto the thread and couch it down to complete the headdress.

Enlarge pattern by 235%

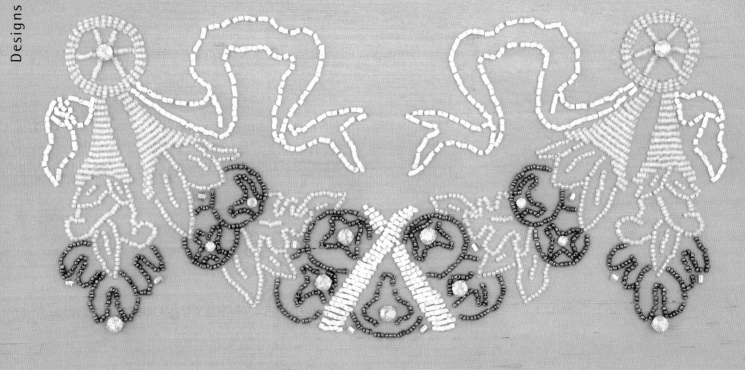

WEDDING GARLAND

Embellishments

30g	10g	15g	15g	9	4	15
26	54	57	117	132	128	1

Stitches

〰〰〰 Couching stitch

〜〜 Satin stitch

--- Running stitch

—— Backstitch

Enlarge pattern by 227%

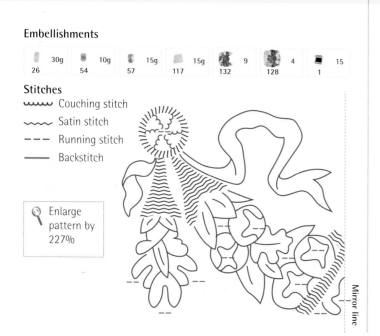

Mirror line

Dimensions 11 x 5 in (28 x 12.5cm)

Applications This wedding garland is inspired by lavish floral arrangements seen at formal weddings. It will sit well on the bodice front of a wedding gown as a neckline treatment, or at the small of the back to form the top frame for a bustle effect on the skirt.

Method Begin by satin-stitching the opalescent seed beads in the areas denoted on the pattern, noting the direction of the stitching. Sew the Swarovski stones into position with running stitch and then make the "spokes" in the circular parts of the motif with couch-stitched opalescent seed beads. Outline the leaves on the garland with silver-white and opalescent seed beads using multiple beads on a backstitch—2 beads per stitch. Outline the flowers with pearlescent gray seed beads using the same stitch. Satin-stitch the two-cut beads on the crossed ribbon of the garland, and then sprinkle on the 6/0 silver seed beads, using running stitch. Finally, outline the trailing ribbons with the two-cut beads using multiple beads on a backstitch—2 beads per stitch.

Embellishments

94	57	60
5g	20g	5g

26	152	132
40g	7	8

128	117
7	15g

Stitches

〰〰〰 Couching stitch

〜〜〜 Satin stitch

- - - Running stitch

——— Backstitch

o–o–o Sequins on a running
stitch

Dimensions 14 1/4 x 8 in (36.5 x 20.5cm)

Applications This lavish, V-shaped motif is just right for the front bodice of a wedding gown. It works well as the focal point on V-neck and round necklines. You could also scale up the motif to trim the train on the skirt.

Method First sew on the 9mm translucent sequins with sequins on a running stitch, working from the scroll outward to the center. Outline the areas noted on the diagram with the pearlescent gray seed beads using multiple beads on a backstitch—3 beads per stitch—and then sew on the 3mm flat sequins with sequins on a running stitch. Fill in the areas indicated on the diagram with the opalescent seed beads in satin stitch, and then sew the 10mm, 8mm, and 4mm Swarovski stones into position. Finally, outline the trailing ribbons with couch-stitched two-cut beads.

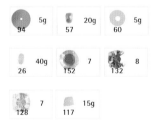

Mirror line

🔍 Enlarge pattern by 200%

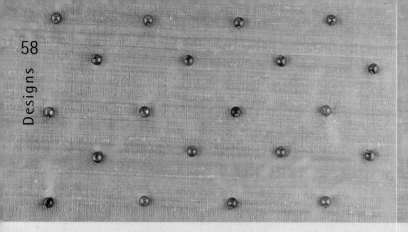

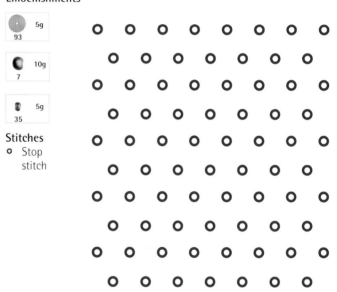

STEP AND REPEAT 1

Embellishments

 10g
120

10g
27

Stitches
o Stop
   stitch

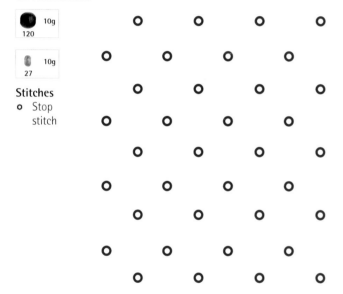

Enlarge pattern by 300%

Dimensions 7 x 7 in (18 x 18cm). This fill is done on a 2 in (5cm) grid, but can be scaled up or down easily.
Applications This step and repeat pattern is a classic way of filling space, either large areas on a garment, or smaller areas between motifs.
Method Sew on the 6mm purple beads individually using stop stitch, with the 11/0 seed beads as the stop beads. Knot off after every three or four stitches without breaking the thread, to prevent an entire section from unraveling if one bead breaks off.

STEP AND REPEAT 2

Embellishments

5g
93

10g
7

 5g
35

Stitches
o Stop
   stitch

Enlarge pattern by 290%

Dimensions 7 x 7 in (18 x 18cm) This fill is done on a 2 in (5cm) grid, but can be scaled up or down easily.
Applications This variation on the step and repeat is a little more dramatic than Step and Repeat 1 (see left) because of the inclusion of the sequins, which create sparkle in movement.
Method Sew on the 6/0 gold seed beads and 9mm sequins individually using stop stitch, using the 11/0 seed beads as the stop beads. Knot off after every three or four stitches without breaking the thread, to prevent an entire section from unraveling if one bead breaks off.

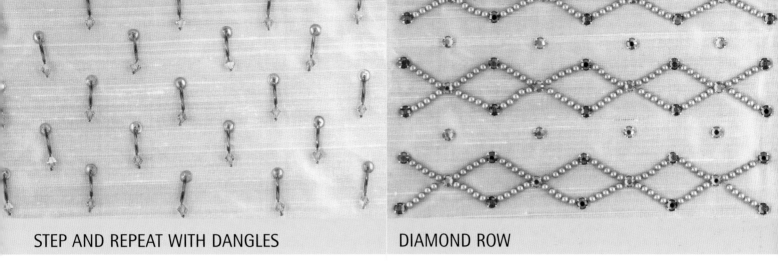

STEP AND REPEAT WITH DANGLES

DIAMOND ROW

Embellishments

89	1ps
50	3ps
110	1ps
142	1ps

Stitches

///// Dangle stitch

Embellishments

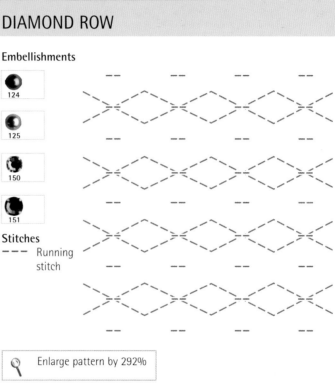

124	
125	
150	
151	

Stitches

--- Running stitch

🔍 Enlarge pattern by 294%

🔍 Enlarge pattern by 292%

Dimensions 8 x 7 in (20 x 18cm) There are approximately 5 dangles per 2 x 2 in (5 x 5cm). Use the amounts listed above per stitch (ps).

Applications Dangles enhance the step and repeat pattern and give movement to the piece. The beads used on the dangles can vary to taste. Be creative!

Method Sew the beads on with dangle stitch. Thread on a sequin, then an 11/0 seed bead, then a bugle bead, another 11/0 seed bead, the Swarovski 6mm faceted bead, and finally an 11/0 seed bead as the stop bead. Knot off after every stitch without breaking the thread to make the work more secure.

Dimensions 8¼ x 7½ in (21 x 19cm) This fill is worked on a 1 in (2.5cm) grid, offset halfway. You can scale it up easily but you will need to use more 4mm pearls between the stones to make the fill.

Applications Ideal for pieces that have a geometric style—the pattern lends itself to op-art clothing or home furnishings.

Method Use Nymo thread as it is more durable. Use running stitch to attach the topaz and smoked topaz stones where indicated, ensuring that the channels on the backs of the stones are running square to the grid. Work the 4mm pearl beads between each topaz and smoked topaz stone by stringing 5 beads on a thread and attaching them by passing the thread through the channels on the back of the topaz and smoked topaz stones.

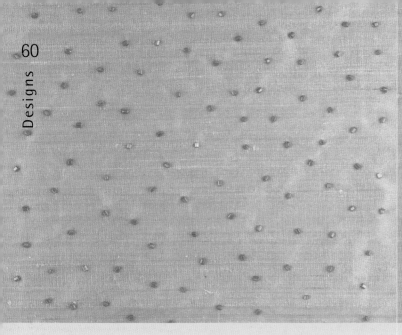

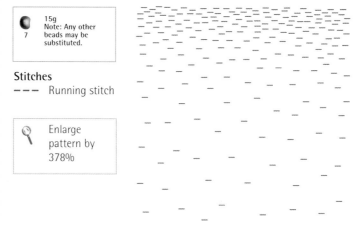

RANDOM SCATTER: EVEN

RANDOM SCATTER: GRADIENT

Embellishments

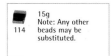

114 | 15g
Note: Any other beads may be substituted.

Embellishments

7 | 15g
Note: Any other beads may be substituted.

Stitches

– – – Running stitch

Stitches

– – – Running stitch

Enlarge pattern by 357%

Enlarge pattern by 378%

Dimensions 8 x 7³/₄ in (20 x 19.5cm) Scales up or down easily and will fill any amount of space.

Applications The random scatter is a beautiful fill, one that creates the pattern of raindrops on a window. It is effective and very versatile as an all-over pattern, its use ranging from evening bags to large evening coats.

Method Stitch as marked on the diagram using running stitch. Knot off the thread without breaking it, every 6 to 8 beads. Examine the pattern closely—you will notice that it is created by making irregular groups of 5 beads, which is the secret to making it look random yet evenly spaced.

Dimensions 7¹/₂ x 7 in (19 x 18cm) Scales up or down easily and will fill any amount of space.

Applications The random scatter gradient can be placed on any angle, and the fade can go in any direction. It is ideal for blending a bead motif or border into a background.

Method Use running stitch to attach the beads, starting with the more closely spaced beads first and working outwards to the more widely spaced areas. With some practice, this can be done without a template.

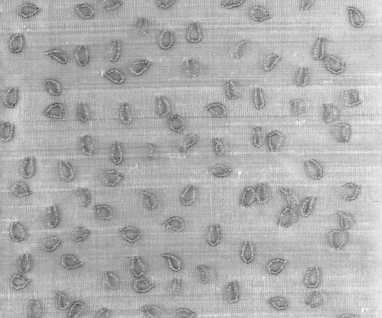

RANDOM SCATTER: BOUCLÉ

WATERFALL

Embellishments

 20g
47

Stitches

〜〜〜 Bouclé stitch

 Enlarge pattern by 345%

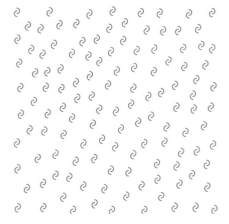

Embellishments

107 40g

35 10g

Stitches

///// Dangle stitch

 Enlarge pattern by 333%

Dimensions 8 x 7 1/2 in (20 x 19cm) Worked on a random scatter grid, this fill can be scaled up or down easily.

Applications This fill gives movement to a work, as well as pattern. The number of beads on the stitch, as well as the choice of bead, can be varied infinitely.

Method Use Nymo thread to bouclé-stitch the beads in place. Keep thread tension slightly loose to make the loops drape nicely. The example shows 15 seed beads per stitch, but you can vary this number or even have a different number of beads on each stitch—the random scatter will facilitate variety in the stitches.

Dimensions 7 1/2 x 7 1/2 in (19 x 19cm) Based on the random scatter: gradient template, this fill can be scaled up or down.

Applications The waterfall is seen in evening clothes and evening bags from the 1920s.

Method Use Nymo thread for this fill, and apply one stitch per dot. For the first row, use 3 bugle beads in each dangle stitch. For the next three rows, use 5, and for all following rows, use 7. Use the light blue seed beads as stop beads. When passing the needle back through the string of gold bugle beads, keep the point of the needle dragging along the inside to prevent sewing through the thread, which creates snarling. Knot off after every 3 stitches for security.

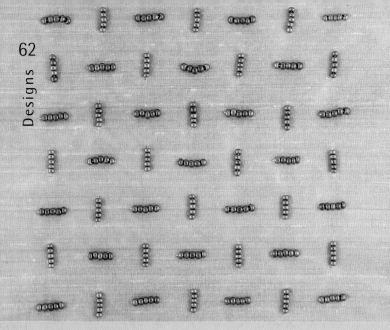

BASKET WEAVE 1

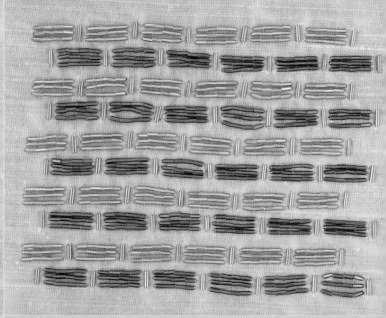

BRICK BASKET WEAVE

Embellishments

6   5g

Stitches

 Multiple beads on a stitch

 Enlarge pattern by 375%

Dimensions 6³/₄ x 6¹/₂ in (17 x 16.5cm) Worked on a 2 in (5cm) grid, this fill scales up and down easily.

Applications Instead of stitching beads on the intersecting points of a grid, beads are stitched at right angles, creating the illusion of a basket weave. This fill works well for geometric motifs, lending an art-deco flavor to the design.

Method Sew this motif with multiple beads on a stitch (5 of the 6/0 seed beads per stitch). Use running stitch to move from one stitch to the next. Knot off after every third or fourth stitch without breaking the thread.

Embellishments

100   20g

101   20g

109   5g

Stitches

--- Running stitch

〜〜 Satin stitch

 Enlarge pattern by 276%

Dimensions 6¹/₄ x 5 in (16 x 12cm)

Applications The brick basket weave is a beautiful fill to enliven an evening bag or the top edges of pockets and cuffs. Use it in combination with other geometric motifs for a stunning composition for an evening bodice or coat.

Method Follow the diagram and attach the 7mm bugle beads with running stitch. Use satin stitch for the dark green bugle beads and work 4 beads to each stitch, then do the same for the light green beads, also working 4 beads to each stitch.

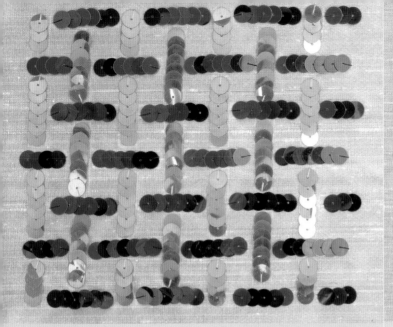

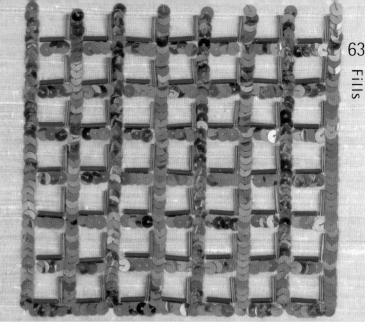

BASKET WEAVE 2

SHADOW BOX GRID

Embellishments

 10g
92

 10g
93

Stitches

○—○—○— Sequins
on a running stitch

 Enlarge
pattern by
400%

Embellishments

 10g
80

▬ 5g
111

Stitches

○—○—○— Sequins on a
running stitch
– – – Running
stitch

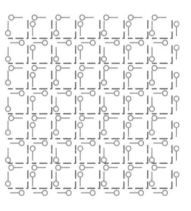 Enlarge
pattern
by 309%

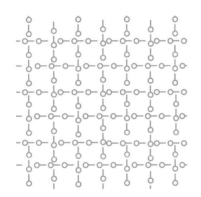

Dimensions 7¹/₄ x 6¹/₄ in (18.5 x 16cm) This fill works on a 2 in (5cm) grid. When scaling up or down, use larger or smaller sequins.
Applications The sequins worked in this pattern would look smart applied all over an evening jacket or vest. The pattern covers lots of the fabric, looks luxurious, and doesn't need any other embellishment.
Method Sew all the sequins using sequins on a running stitch. Color-match the thread to the color of the sequin.

Dimensions 5³/₄ x 5¹/₄ in (14.5 x 13.5cm) Worked on a 2 in (5cm) grid.
Applications The shadow box is another fill that mimics fabric. It is most effective as an all-over fill for a blouse, jacket, or vest.
Method Stitch the sequins with sequins on a running stitch to create the grid. Work the vertical lines first, and work each line in the opposite direction to the last one so that the sequins lie in different directions. Fill in the horizontal spaces in the same stitch, using opposing directions for each line. To finish, sew the bugle beads into the right-hand lower side of each square using running stitch.

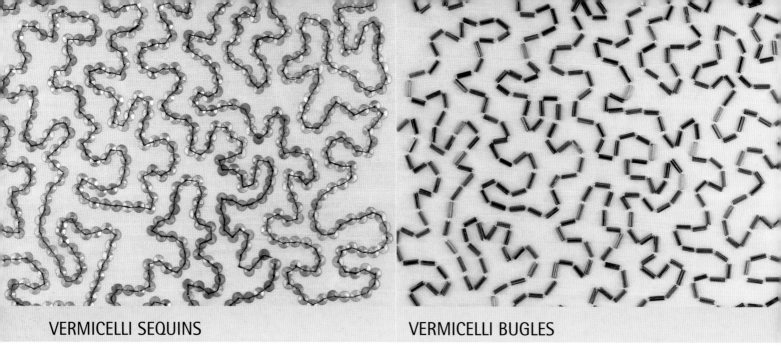

VERMICELLI SEQUINS

Embellishments

 63

(60 sequins per
2 x 2 in
[5 x 5cm])

Stitches

—— Backstitch

 Enlarge pattern by 277%

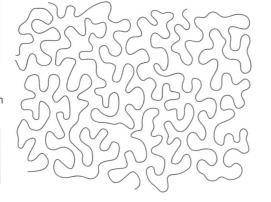

Dimensions 7 x 6 in (18 x 15.5cm) A random pattern that scales up well and easily fills any space.

Applications Vermicelli stitch is generally done "by eye," but using this pattern will give you a feel for how it works. It gives a very pleasing all-over texture, and mixes well when combined with curvilinear motifs, such as flowers.

Method Attach the sequins using backstitch. Make the stitches twice as long, so that the sequins are set edge to edge.

VERMICELLI BUGLES

Embellishments

 106

(40 beads per
2 x 2 in
[5 x 5cm])

Stitches

- - - Running stitch

 Enlarge pattern by 277%

Dimensions 7 x 6 in (18 x 15cm) A random pattern that scales up well and easily fills any space.

Applications The beauty of using this stitch is that it creates the illusion of a more heavily beaded fill. Bob Mackie, the famous Hollywood designer, uses this for his beaded gowns—the all-over sparkle, used to cover an evening top or dress, is the height of luxury.

Method Use running stitch to attach the beads in the pattern, using one bead per stitch.

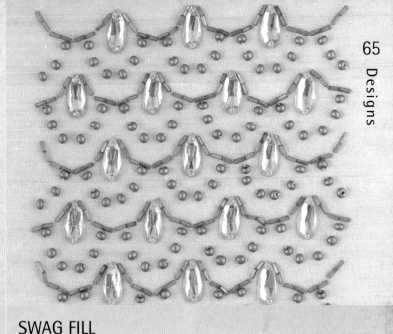

SCALLOP FILL

SWAG FILL

Embellishments

40g 21		13g 69	

Stitches

- ○—○—○ Sequins on a running stitch
- ○ Stop stitch
- ‿‿‿ Couching stitch

1 Repeat

1 Repeat

Enlarge pattern by 264%

Embellishments

17 167		15g 99
15g 7		1g 24

Stitches

- ○ Stop stitch
- - - - Running stitch
- ‿‿‿ Couching stitch

Enlarge pattern by 325%

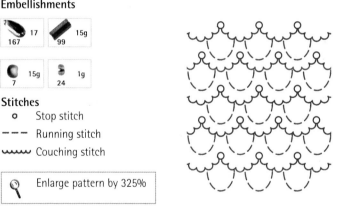

Dimensions 5³/₄ x 5¹/₄ in (14.5 x 13.5cm)
Applications This scallop fill is perfect for a little girl's party dress. Use it on the yoke of the party dress and make matching cuffs.
Method Working row by row, start at the bottom and work up. Sew the pearlescent pink cup sequins, cup-up, along the lines of the scallop using sequins on a running stitch. Next, couch-stitch the pearlescent white beads onto the pattern. Finally, sew a sequin into each scallop as marked using stop stitch with a pearlescent white bead as the stop bead.

Dimensions 5¹/₄ x 5¹/₄ in (13 x 13cm)
Applications The swag fill is a very decorative fill that works well with some of the architectural motifs and borders in this book. Use a border to outline a vest or jacket, and then fill inside the border using the Swag Fill.
Method Sew down the flat-back stones with stop stitch, using the clear seed beads as stop beads. Next, couch-stitch the bugle beads along the scallop lines marked. Finally, use running stitch to attach the 6/0 seed beads in position.

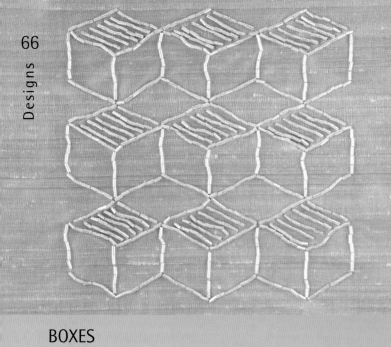

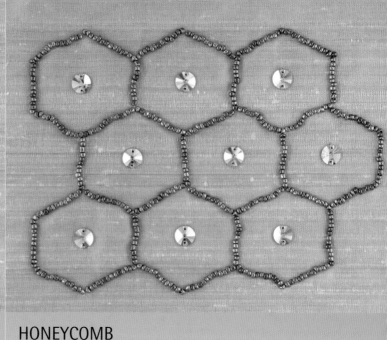

BOXES

HONEYCOMB

Embellishments

20g
104

Stitches

〰〰 Couching stitch

〰 Satin stitch

Enlarge pattern by 250%

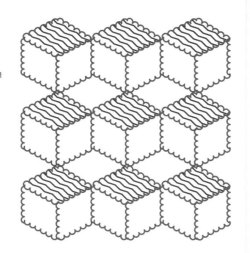

Embellishments

20g
19

163
9

Stitches

〰〰 Couching stitch

--- Running stitch

Enlarge pattern by 277%

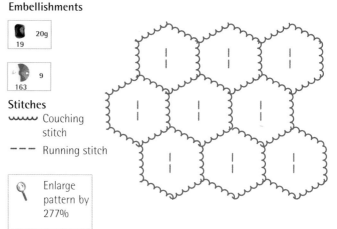

Dimensions 6 x 6 in (15 x 15cm) Worked off a 1 in (2.5cm) triangular grid that scales up easily.
Applications Escher, the artist famous for making patterns that looked like one thing, but appeared to change to another, inspired this fill. Use it to make an all-over pattern on a vest, square handbag, or curtains.
Method Create the outlines of the boxes by couch-stitching the silver bugle beads. Each line of the box will be a separate section of couching stitch. Next, fill in the designated spaces with satin stitch, using 4 bugle beads per stitch. Couch stitch them in the middle for security.

Dimensions 7 x 5¼ in (18 x 13cm) Worked on a 1 in (2.5cm) triangular grid that scales up easily.
Applications The honeycomb is a fill that lends itself to geometric designs. It can fill an entire area and serve as the pattern of the fabric, or you can use it as a background for geometric motifs.
Method Sew the outlines of the honeycomb with couching stitch, using the 8/0 seed beads. Once the outline is complete, sew on the flat-back stones using running stitch—color-match the thread to the color of the stones.

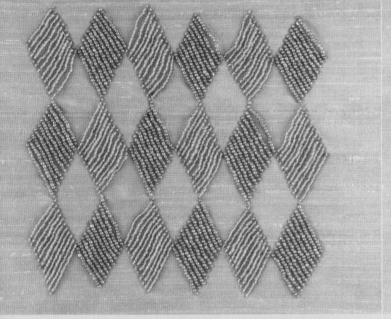

HARLEQUIN

MEDALS

Embellishments

 40g
34

40g
46

Stitches

〜〜〜 Satin stitch

 Enlarge pattern by 291%

Embellishments

20g
95

 9
164

Stitches

〜〜〜 Satin stitch

wwww Couching stitch

- - - Running stitch

 Enlarge pattern by 280%

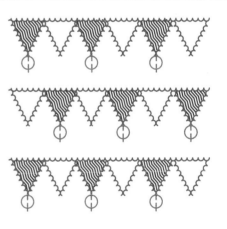

Dimensions 6¹/₄ x 5³/₄ in (16 x 14.5cm) Worked on a 1 in (2.5cm) triangular grid that scales up or down very easily.

Applications The harlequin pattern is a very labor-intensive fill, so use it in small areas, such as the outside of evening bags, collars and cuffs, or for hatbands.

Method Work this pattern in satin stitch, couching it in the middle of the motif for security. Follow the photograph to see the direction of the stitches—the blue seed beads run in the opposite direction to the orange seed beads.

Dimensions 6 x 5¹/₂ in (15.5 x 14cm) Worked on a 1 in (2.5cm) triangular grid.

Applications This fill is like a textile design. It is relatively labor-intensive, so you might consider it for pockets on a jacket or for a handbag.

Method Couch-stitch the 2mm bugle beads to outline every other triangle. Sew the triangles between the beads in satin stitch with the same 2mm bugle beads. Note the direction of the satin stitch in the photograph—all the stitches run in the same direction. Use running stitch to attach the 12mm flat-back stones below the points of the satin-stitch triangles.

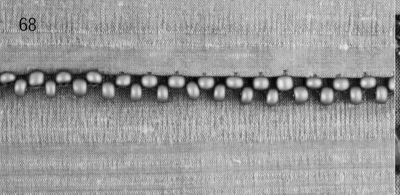

BASIC EDGING STITCH

DANGLE EDGING

Embellishments

7	15g Note: You can substitute any size round-shaped bead, from very small to very large.

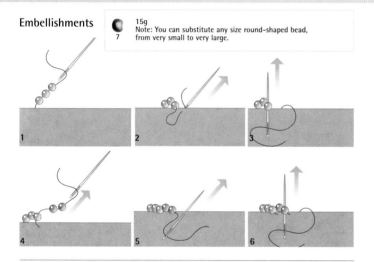

Embellishments

140 → 50	147 → 10	51 → 10g	104 → 10g

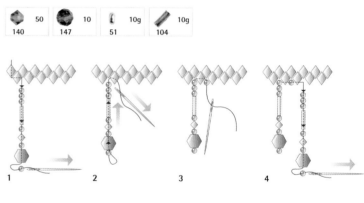

Dimensions 8 in (20cm) Can be worked to any length.

Applications This edge is a beautiful way to add sparkle, as well as weight, to the hem of a dress, the edge of a scarf, or the edges of collars and cuffs.

Method

1 The first step is different from the subsequent steps. After securing the thread on the edge of the fabric with a tiny knot, thread on 3 beads.

2 Insert the needle into the edge of the fabric, just catching the fabric. The stitch length (between the knot and the first stitch) is the length of 1 bead.

3 Without passing through the fabric, insert the needle back up through the end bead and pull the stitch closed.

4 All subsequent stitches are different from the first stitch. Pick up 2 beads on the thread.

5 The stitch length being the same (1 bead length), catch the edge of the fabric with the needle and pull the thread.

6 Without passing through the fabric, insert the needle back up through the end bead and pull the stitch closed. Pick up 2 more beads, and repeat as needed.

Dimensions 4 in (10cm) Can be worked to any length.

Applications This stitch gives a beautiful finish to the ends of scarves, because it gives weight and sparkle.

Method Begin this edge by making the Basic Edging Stitch described left, using the 4mm Swarovski faceted beads. Once the edge is in place, you are ready to make the dangles.

1 Secure the thread to the edge, and then pass the needle up through the last 2 beads. String on your dangle beads—in this case, 3 seed beads, 1 bugle bead, 1 seed bead, 1 4mm faceted bead, 1 seed bead, and 1 8mm faceted bead. Then pick up 1 more seed bead for the stop bead.

2 Pass the needle back through the dangle and pull the stitch closed. Pass the needle through 1 of the 4mm faceted beads on the edging stitch.

3 Pick up a seed bead and then pass the needle through another of the 4mm faceted beads.

4 Make another dangle, as you did in Step 1, then repeat Steps 2 and 3.

BASIC WHIP STITCH

CHAIN STITCH EDGE

Embellishments

| 51 | 5g |

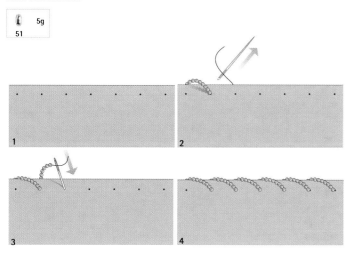

Embellishments

| 51 | 20g | 37 | 20g |

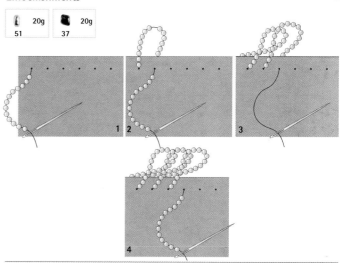

Dimensions 4$\frac{1}{2}$ in (12cm)
Applications Whip stitches are useful for embellishing an existing garment.
Method
1 Mark the dots onto the edge to be sewn. The spacing can be any size you desire, but here it is $\frac{1}{2}$ in (1.5cm) apart, and $\frac{1}{4}$ in (0.5cm) from the edge.
2 After securing your thread into the fabric, thread on 14 to 15 of the 11/0 gold seed beads per stitch (enough to cover the fabric edges), and then insert the needle onto the mark.
3 Pull the thread closed.
4 Thread the same number of seed beads on the thread again, and then insert the needle into the next mark.

Dimensions 7 in (18.5cm) Can be worked to any length.
Applications This stitch is inspired by the edge that is used in tooled leather working. It would make a beautiful edge for lapels on a semi-formal jacket for evening, or for hostess gowns.
Method Mark your dots for spacing—this example uses dots that are $\frac{1}{2}$ in (1.5cm) apart and $\frac{1}{4}$ in (0.5cm) from the edge. There are 45 beads per stitch, and two different colors are used, to show the individual stitches.
1 Secure the thread at the back of the fabric on the first mark. Thread on 45 seed beads in the first color.
2 Insert the needle into the fabric and pull the stitch closed. Thread on 45 seed beads in the second color.
3 Twist the first loop and bring the needle with the second set of beads through the top of the twist. Bring the needle through the back of the fabric, pinning the first loop to the fabric (secure this with a stitch later), and creating a second loop.
4 Thread on 45 seed beads, first color, and continue in the same way. The completed stitch looks like a chain stitch.

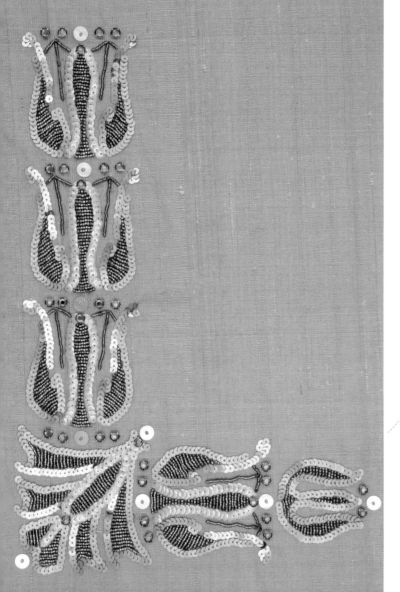

TULIP BORDER

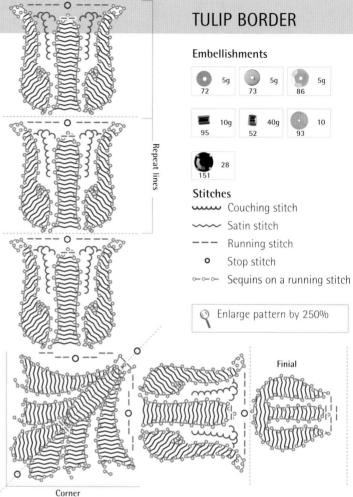

Embellishments

72	5g	73	5g	86	5g
95	10g	52	40g	93	10
151	28				

Stitches

〜〜〜〜 Couching stitch

〜〜〜 Satin stitch

- - - Running stitch

○ Stop stitch

○—○—○ Sequins on a running stitch

🔍 Enlarge pattern by 250%

Repeat lines

Finial

Corner

Dimensions 14 (length of longest side shown) x 3¹/₄ (width) in (35.5 x 8cm)
Applications Enjoy the abstract quality of this tulip border by applying it to the edges of a lavish table runner. If finished beautifully, it could double as an evening shawl.
Method This design has three parts: the repeat, the finial, and the corner. Since it is a directional design, you will want to mirror-image the repeats at the center of the work, so the repeats will line up with the corners. The finial gives you the choice of ending the border with a different but coordinating motif.

Working from the tips of the flowers toward the base, use sequins on a running stitch to sew the 4mm matte gold sequins, then the bright gold sequins, and finally the 6mm translucent sequins cup-down. Fill in the spaces noted on the diagram with the iridescent gold seed beads in satin stitch, and then couch-stitch the copper bugle beads in place. Sew on the smoked topaz roses montées with running stitch and finish by sewing on the 9mm gold sequins with stop stitch, using iridescent gold seed beads as stop beads.

RIBBON LATTICE BORDER

Embellishments

● 3g **80**	⊙ 6g **92**	✳ 4 **132**
✱ 8 **130**	▮ 50g **5**	▮ 40g **3**

Stitches

〜〜〜 Satin stitch

○–○–○ Sequins on a running stitch

– – – Running stitch

∞∞∞∞ Chain stitch

⌒⌒⌒⌒ Couching stitch

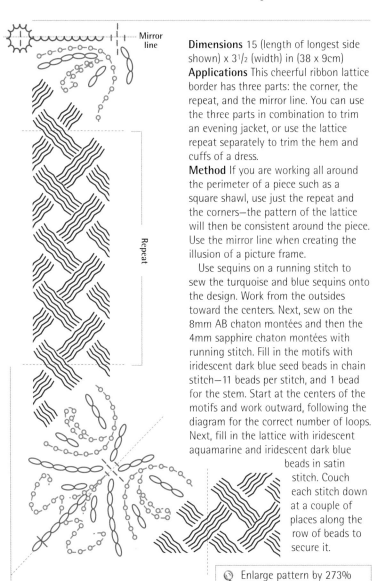

Mirror line

Repeat

Corner

Dimensions 15 (length of longest side shown) x 3^1/$_2$ (width) in (38 x 9cm)

Applications This cheerful ribbon lattice border has three parts: the corner, the repeat, and the mirror line. You can use the three parts in combination to trim an evening jacket, or use the lattice repeat separately to trim the hem and cuffs of a dress.

Method If you are working all around the perimeter of a piece such as a square shawl, use just the repeat and the corners—the pattern of the lattice will then be consistent around the piece. Use the mirror line when creating the illusion of a picture frame.

Use sequins on a running stitch to sew the turquoise and blue sequins onto the design. Work from the outsides toward the centers. Next, sew on the 8mm AB chaton montées and then the 4mm sapphire chaton montées with running stitch. Fill in the motifs with iridescent dark blue seed beads in chain stitch—11 beads per stitch, and 1 bead for the stem. Start at the centers of the motifs and work outward, following the diagram for the correct number of loops. Next, fill in the lattice with iridescent aquamarine and iridescent dark blue beads in satin stitch. Couch each stitch down at a couple of places along the row of beads to secure it.

🔍 Enlarge pattern by 273%

BRIDAL ROSE VINE

Embellishments

117	50g	54	30g
87	3g	2	5g

🔍 Enlarge pattern by 318%

Stitches

〰️ Satin stitch

o Stop stitch

— Backstitch

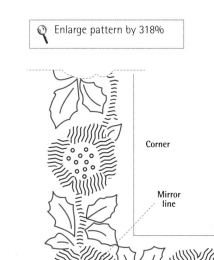

Corner

Mirror line

Dimensions 18$^{1}/_{2}$ (length of longest side shown) x 2$^{1}/_{4}$ (width) in (47 x 6cm)

Applications The bridal rose vine is an elegant border suited to trimming the neckline, cuffs, and waistline of an Empire-style gown. The blossoms can be separated out and scattered across the bodice or skirt of the bridal gown. The border can also be worked as an appliqué to create the headpiece for the bridal veil.

Method This is a two-part border composed of the repeat and the corner. The corner has the mirror line, meaning that the repeat shown will be mirror-imaged to join the opposite side of the corner.

First satin-stitch the petals of the flowers with the two-cut beads. Outline the leaves with 11/0 silver-white seed beads using multiple beads on a backstitch—3 beads per stitch—and then finish the vines with the same beads in satin stitch. Finally, finish the centers of the flowers by sewing on the cup sequins (cup-up) with stop stitch, using the 6/0 seed beads as stop beads.

Repeat

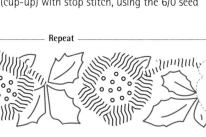

FAMILY TIES

Embellishments

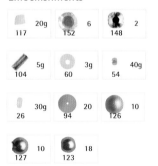

20g 117	6 152	2 148
5g 104	3g 60	40g 54
30g 26	20 94	10 126
10 127	18 123	

Stitches

- – – – Running stitch
- 〜〜 Satin stitch
- o Stop stitch
- ᴡᴡᴡ Couching stitch
- o–o–o Sequins on a running stitch

Dimensions 15$\frac{1}{4}$ (length of longest side shown) x 3$\frac{1}{2}$ (width) in (38.5 x 9cm)

Applications This elaborate bridal border would be beautiful trimming the neckline, cuffs, and hem of a bridal gown. The "frames" in the border are left blank for incorporating such motifs as religious symbols, the bride's monogram, or good luck symbols. Use the repeat as an appliqué to make a stunning headdress for the wedding veil.

Method This is a two-part border composed of the repeat and the corner. Begin by working the "frames," then the ribbon in the swag with the two-cut beads in satin stitch. Next, sew on the 10mm and 8mm roses montées stones with running stitch, and then embroider the leaves of the swag with the 3mm flat sequins, using sequins on a running stitch. Finish the base of the leaves with couch-stitched silver bugle beads. Satin-stitch the ribbons beside the "frames" using the 11/0 seed beads—first the silver-white seed beads, then the opalescent glass seed beads. To finish, sew the 9mm flat sequins around the 8mm roses montées using running stitch—these should resemble the petals of flowers when finished.

Finally, sew the 6mm white and gray pearls and 4mm gray pearls into position using stop stitch, with silver-white seed beads as stop beads.

Enlarge pattern by 310%

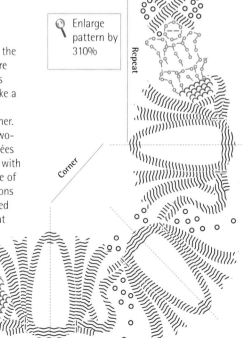

Repeat

Corner

Repeat

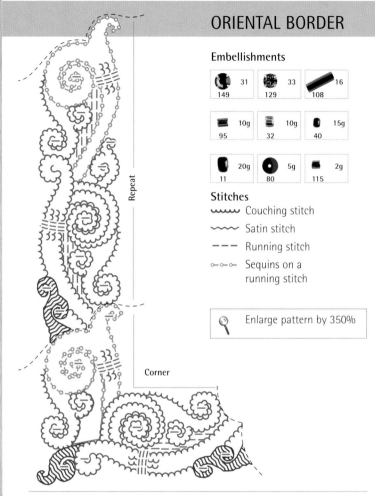

ORIENTAL BORDER

Embellishments

31	33	16			
149	129	108			
10g	10g	15g			
95	32	40			
20g	5g	2g			
11	80	115			

Stitches

〰〰〰 Couching stitch

〰〰 Satin stitch

- - - Running stitch

o–o–o Sequins on a running stitch

🔍 Enlarge pattern by 350%

Repeat

Corner

Dimensions 17³/₄ (length of longest side shown) x 3¹/₄ (width) in (45cm x 8cm)

Applications Evoke the mystery of the Far East with this beaded border, which would look beautiful on a long shawl or scarf. Trim the hem of a gown with it as well, for a coordinated effect.

Method This design has two parts, the repeat and the corner, which means when it is placed around a square it will travel in one direction without a "mirror image." The diagram indicates where the repeats join. The corner joins the repeats in the same way.

Use running stitch to sew down the 8mm roses montées and then the 4mm chaton montées and the blue-green bugle beads. Next, couch-stitch the 2mm copper bugle beads to the motif, and then the 11/0 iridescent aquamarine seed beads. Satin-stitch the 11/0 dark purple seed beads into the areas indicated, and then couch-stitch the 6/0 copper seed beads, sewing the two outlines first, then the line between them. Sew the sequins on with sequins on a running stitch, starting at the tips of the motif and working down to the base. Finally, randomly scatter the two-cut brown beads in the marked areas using running stitch.

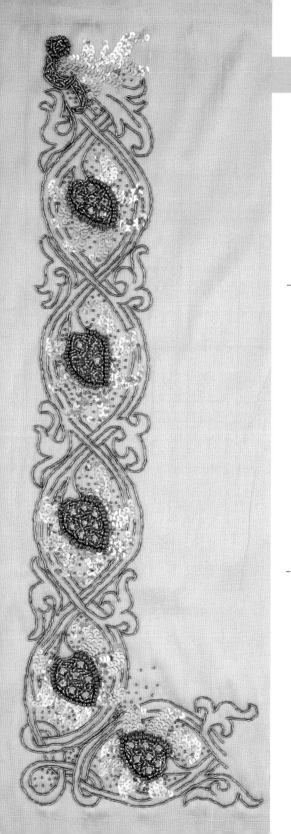

GOLDEN SUNFLOWER BORDER

Embellishments

40g	35	10g			
95	149	73			
20g	20g	5g			
11	52	58			

Stitches

〰〰〰 Couching stitch

∘–∘–∘ Sequins on a running stitch

∿∿∿ Bouclé stitch

– – – Running stitch

🔍 Enlarge pattern by 292%

Dimensions 22³/₄ (length of longest side shown) x 3¹/₂ (width) in (58 x 9cm)

Applications Evoking the gilded frame of an old oil painting, this magnificent, elaborate border would be perfect for trimming the edges of a simple cardigan-style jacket and cuffs.

Method This border has three parts: The corner, the repeat, and the center motif. The corner and the center motifs mirror along their center lines, making this border work around a square in sections.

Couch-stitch the 2mm bugle beads on the outlines, then sew sequins with sequins on a running stitch to the petals and the other sequin areas indicated on the diagram. Work from the tips of the petals to the center of the flower, and from the edges toward the center of the petals. Sew on the roses montées with running stitch. Border the centers of the flowers by couch-stitching the 6/0 copper seed beads. Fill inside the border, around the roses montées, with iridescent gold seed beads in bouclé stitch, using 5 beads per stitch. Finally, use running stitch to scatter the gunmetal gray seed beads between the petals.

Center motif

Repeat

Corner

DENTIL BORDER

WAVES

Embellishments

3g 78	5g 93	30g 9

Stitches

∞∞∞ Chain stitch

∘−∘−∘ Sequins on a running stitch

᳁᳁᳁ Multiple beads on a stitch

Corner

Repeat

🔍 Enlarge pattern by 188%

Embellishments

50g 52

Stitches

᳁᳁᳁ Couching stitch

🔍 Enlarge pattern by 188%

Repeat line

Dimensions 7 (length of longest side shown) x 2¹/₄ (width) in (18 x 6cm)
Applications This tailored border is perfect for trimming a jacket hem and the short repeat makes it possible to trim matching pocket flaps, cuffs, and collar. Dentil is an architectural term referring to a small, tooth-shaped block used as a repeating ornament in a cornice.
Method The border has two parts, the repeat and the corner. It is adaptable to curves because of the open nature of the pattern. First, sew the 5mm dark green sequins and then the 9mm gold sequins using sequins on a running stitch. Fill in the areas marked on the diagram with 6/0 seed beads in chain stitch, starting at the gold sequins. Use 11 beads per loop and 1 bead for the stem. Work 6 chain loops per row and finish the row by couching down the last loop, using multiple beads (5) on a stitch. For the outer corner, work 4 loops from each end so they meet at the middle. At the inner corner, 1 loop is sufficient.

Dimensions 8³/₄ x 3 in (22.5 x 7.5cm)
Applications This rich but simple border works well on sleeve edges and hems, or on the ends of a shawl—the weight of the beads will give it a pleasing hang and drape.
Method This border consists of a single repeat and the entire piece is couch-stitched. The beads are strung on the thread and laid in like a satin stitch, but because they are extremely long, couch-stitch the rows down next to each other, stitching every 4 to 5 beads to keep them in position.

TORNADO BORDER

Embellishments

 44 20g 81 5g 151 4

Stitches

—— Backstitch

- - - Running stitch

🔍 Enlarge pattern by 200%

Dimensions 9³/₄ x 2¹/₄ in (24.5 x 6cm)

Applications This dramatic border has lots of sparkle. It is effective when used for edging cuffs and hems but would be most dynamic worked in multiple vertical rows on an evening skirt.

Method This is a simple repeat border. The main stitching is a variation of large and small beads on a backstitch but, instead of using large beads, use sequins. The first stitch is different from the rest.

Step 1 Thread on 1 sequin, cup-up, then 5 seed beads, then another sequin cup-up. Stitch into the fabric so that the sequins sit edge to edge. Close the stitch.

Step 2 Carry the needle under the fabric and emerge on the design line, making the stitch the diameter of the sequin so the sequins sit edge to edge. Thread on 1 sequin cup-up and 5 seed beads.

Step 3 Insert the needle into the hole of the previous sequin and pull the stitch closed.

Step 4 Repeat steps 2 and 3.

After working this stitch along the lines, sew the roses montées into position using running stitch.

Repeat line

HELIX

Embellishments

159 25 32 10g 5 40g

Stitches

—— Backstitch

∞∞∞ Chain stitch

🔍 Enlarge pattern by 154%

Dimensions 8³/₄ x 2¹/₄ in (22.5 x 6cm)

Applications Sometimes a simple border is needed to accentuate an elegantly cut garment. This border provides the right combination of simplicity and richness. Imagine it in a vertical row along the side seams of evening trousers.

Method This border consists of the repeat only. Work the pearl sections first with large and small beads on a backstitch using the 8mm pearls and 5 of the 11/0 seed beads for each stitch. Next, sew the line of 6/0 iridescent dark blue seed beads in chain stitch—each loop has 9 seed beads and 1 bead for the stem. The short loop produces a braid-like effect.

Repeat line

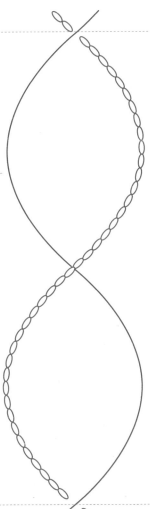

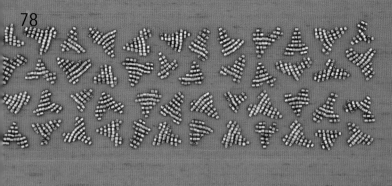

PATINA

Embellishments

20g 32	20g 56		

Stitches

〜〜〜 Satin stitch

Dimensions 8 x 2¼ in
(20.5 x 6cm)

Applications This abstract border functions texturally, evoking the beauty of patinated metal. Use it for edges or run it side by side and end to end to fill an area.

Method This is a simple repeat border that is easy to work as it is all in satin stitch. Follow the diagram to see where to use the different colored beads. There is no uniform direction for the satin stitching—angle the satin stitch in a different direction for each part of the border. This will help to accentuate the patinated metal effect.

Repeat line

🔍 Enlarge pattern by 167%

NEO-GOTHIC

Embellishments

3g 78	3g 73	10g 42
15g 8	4 149	3 129
5g 106		

Stitches

--- Running stitch

〜〜〜 Satin stitch

o–o–o– Sequins on a running stitch

 🔍 Enlarge pattern by 227%

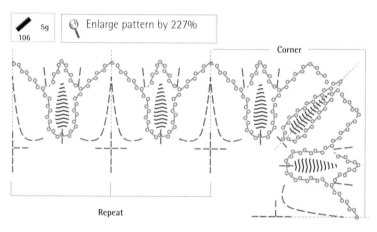

Corner

Repeat

Dimensions 6 (length of longest side shown) x 2¼ (width) in
(15.5 x 5.5cm)

Applications This Neo-Gothic border evokes the embellishment of Gothic architecture. Use it to edge table linens, altar cloths, or ecclesiastical garments—any item that requires richness but not ostentation.

Method This two-part border is composed of the repeat and the corner. First, sew on the dark green sequins using sequins on a running stitch—work from the points downward. Next, outline the shorter points with 4mm gold sequins, also working from the point downward. Fill in the teardrop-shaped areas with satin-stitched pink-blue seed beads, running the stitches as shown in the diagram. Use running stitch to sew the 6/0 gold seed beads onto the border and to attach the Swarovski stones, first the 8mm and then the 4mm, and finally to sew the 6mm bugle beads in place.

EGG AND DART

SAPPHIRE BRACELET

Embellishments

40	49	51	149
40g	40g	30g	5

Stitches

- - -   Running stitch

〜〜〜   Satin stitch

〰〰〰   Couching stitch

🔍 Enlarge pattern by 183%

Dimensions 9³/₄ (length of longest side shown) x 2¹/₄ (width) in (24.5 x 5.5cm)
Applications The egg and dart is a classic motif used in Ancient Greece and in Beaux Arts architecture. This restrained and dignified interpretation would be beautiful for trimming home furnishings or decorating the cuffs of a dressing gown.
Method This is a two-part border composed of the repeat and the corner. You work it almost entirely in satin stitch except for couching any strands of satin stitch that are too long to lie flat. Use the different colors as indicated in the photograph and stitch in the directions shown to achieve the contrast in texture. Finish the border by sewing on the 8mm roses montées to the points of the darts using running stitch.

Embellishments

130	83
80	10g

Stitches

- - -   Running stitch

∘–∘–∘   Sequins on a running stitch

Dimensions 6³/₄ x 2 in (17 x 5cm)
Applications The sapphire bracelet border is simple in design but derives its richness from the extravagant use of materials. As its name suggests, this border is best used as a trim for cuffs and neckline, making any jewelry unnecessary.
Method This is a two-part border composed of the repeat and the end. Begin by sewing the 4mm chaton montées down the center of the motif with running stitch, placing each chaton monté close to the next. Next, fill in the rows of flat sequins on either side of the chaton montées using sequins on a running stitch. Sew them on the lines indicated to create the illusion of a twisting border.

🔍 Enlarge pattern by 142%

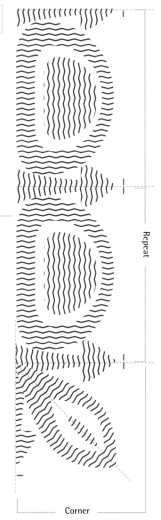

Corner

Repeat

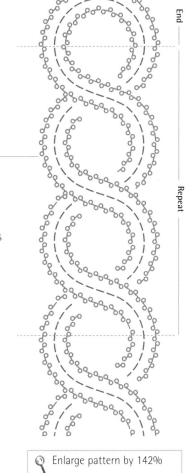

End

Repeat

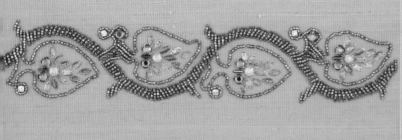

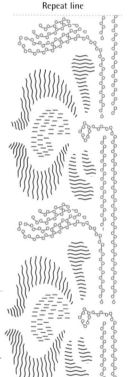

AUTUMN LEAVES

Embellishments

| 131 | 4 | 151 | 10 | 150 | 4 |

| 108 | 4 | 52 | 20g | 91 | 40 |

Stitches
- - - Running stitch

〜〜 Satin stitch

——— Multiple beads on
a backstitch

🔍 Enlarge pattern by 198%

Dimensions 10 x 1³/₄ in (25 x 4.5cm)
Applications This autumn leaves border is
unidirectional and suitable for trimming long lengths
of edging, such as the hem of a voluminous taffeta
evening skirt and matching shawl.
Method This border consists of a single repeat. First
sew on the 4mm chaton montées, then the smoked
topaz and topaz roses montées, and finally the bugle
beads using running stitch. Next, outline the leaves
and chaton montées on the branches with 11/0
iridescent gold seed beads using multiple beads on a
backstitch—3 beads per stitch. Fill in the vine using
the same beads in satin stitch. Finally, fill in the
leaves with the 8 x 4mm navette-shaped sequins
using running stitch. Sew a stitch in the holes at
both ends of each sequin.

Repeat line

BEARDED IRIS

Embellishments

| 135 | 76 | 77 | 5g |

| 41 | 10g | 40 | 20g |

Stitches
- - - Running stitch

〜〜 Satin stitch

o–o–o Sequins on a running
stitch

🔍 Enlarge pattern by 227%

Repeat line

Dimensions 8³/₄ x 2³/₄ in (22.5 x 7cm)
Applications The bearded iris is a beautiful
and exotic flower but very perishable.
This iris border will remain lovely for all time—
trim a spring frock with bands of irises at the
waist and hem.
Method This border consists of a single repeat.
First sew on the sequins using sequins on a running stitch, working the top
rows from right to left and the leaves from tip to base. Work the lower row
from left to right and the stem of the flower from bottom to top. Next, fill
in the lower petals with satin-stitched iridescent purple seed beads and fill
in the upper petals with satin-stitched dark purple seed beads. Finally, fill
in the center petals with the lochrosen using running stitch—space them
randomly by eye to fill in the space.

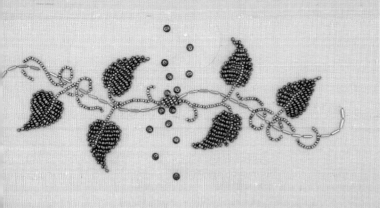

IVY

Embellishments

● 138	14	▬ 106	6g
▮ 28	10g	▮ 22	15g

Stitches

- – – – Running stitch
- 〜〜〜 Satin stitch
- ◦◦◦ Multiple beads on a stitch
- ○ Stop stitch

🔍 Enlarge pattern by 211%

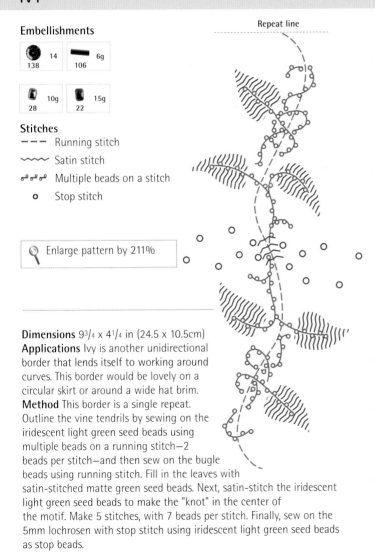

Repeat line

Dimensions 9³/₄ x 4¹/₄ in (24.5 x 10.5cm)
Applications Ivy is another unidirectional border that lends itself to working around curves. This border would be lovely on a circular skirt or around a wide hat brim.
Method This border is a single repeat. Outline the vine tendrils by sewing on the iridescent light green seed beads using multiple beads on a running stitch—2 beads per stitch—and then sew on the bugle beads using running stitch. Fill in the leaves with satin-stitched matte green seed beads. Next, satin-stitch the iridescent light green seed beads to make the "knot" in the center of the motif. Make 5 stitches, with 7 beads per stitch. Finally, sew on the 5mm lochrosen with stop stitch using iridescent light green seed beads as stop beads.

PEONY AND SCROLLS

Embellishments

▮ 18	7g	▮ 29	7g	◉ 73	5g

Stitches

- ◦–◦–◦ Sequins on a running stitch
- —— Backstitch

🔍 Enlarge pattern by 180%

Repeat line

Dimensions 10 x 2 in (25 x 5cm)
Applications The peony and scrolls is another springtime border, but this one is perfect for evening wear—try it as a trim for the neckline of an evening blouse.
Method This is a unidirectional single repeat border. First, sew on the sequins using sequins on a running stitch, working the rows of sequins from the tips of the scrolls to the base. Fill the entire area, overlapping slightly to get the proper coverage. Next, sew on the 8/0 pink seed beads and the 11/0 iridescent dark green seed beads using multiple beads on a backstitch—2 beads per pink stitch and 3 beads per green stitch.

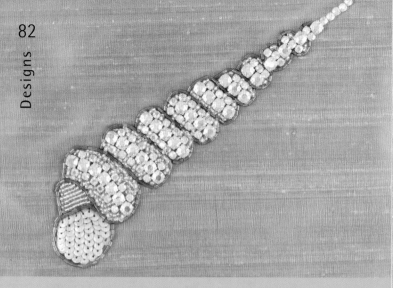

QUILL SHELL

Embellishments

35		60		10g		20g		3g	Enlarge pattern by 182%
132		128		97		53		74	

Stitches

〰 Couching stitch

--- Running stitch

∿∿∿ Bouclé stitch

〜 Satin stitch

⊸∘⊸ Sequins on a running stitch

Dimensions 8 x 2 in (20 x 5cm)
Applications This glittery quill shell on the lapel of an evening jacket will be all the jewelry you need.
Method Use running stitch to sew in place the 8mm chaton montées and the 4mm chaton montées. Couch-stitch the gray bugle beads to make the outlines of the shell design, and then fill the area between the chaton montées and the bugle beads with silver seed beads using bouclé stitch with 5 beads per stitch. Next, satin-stitch silver seed beads to fill in the lower body of the shell. Finally, use sequins on a running stitch to sew matte silver cup sequins, cup-down, to make the inside of the shell opening. Work the rows from the center outward.

JUNE BUG

Embellishments

6		26		2		5g		
148		129		128		119		
4		1g		5g		3g		
12		84		53		80		

Stitches

〰 Couching stitch

--- Running stitch

⊸∘⊸ Sequins on a running stitch

∿∿∿ Bouclé stitch

〜 Satin stitch

	Enlarge pattern by 220%

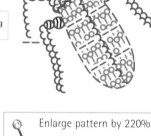

Dimensions 4$\frac{1}{2}$ x 3$\frac{1}{4}$ in (11 x 8cm)
Applications This cheerful little June bug would look very witty perched on the shoulder of a jacket for day or evening wear.
Method Couch-stitch the two-cut black beads to outline the body, antennae, wings, and legs, and then fill the tops of the legs with the same beads using satin stitch. Next, make the head by stitching 6mm black cup sequins, cup-down, with sequins on a running stitch. Sew in a spiral pattern, starting in the center. Use running stitch to sew on the 6/0 black seed beads for the feet and to top the antennae with the AB chaton montées. Couch-stitch the silver outline on the thorax with silver seed beads and bouclé-stitch the same beads, using 5 beads per stitch, to fill this area. Fill the upper thorax with the 4mm padparadscha chaton montées using running stitch and fill any large gaps between the chaton montées with silver seed beads worked in bouclé stitch. Use sequins on a running stitch to fill the wings with 5mm turquoise flat sequins—work from the tips of the wings up toward the thorax, and work from the center line outward. Finally, sew down the roses montées onto the wings using running stitch. Pass the needle up through the holes in the sequins to do this.

FLORAL URN

Embellishments

20	11	15g	1g	
151	131	9	72	

15g	Buttons, single earrings, odd beads, and any other pretty objects that could compose a fantasy floral arrangement
11	

Stitches

〰〰 Couching stitch

--- Running stitch

o-o-o Sequins on a running stitch

🔍 Enlarge pattern by 267%

Dimensions 8 x 4 in (20 x 10.5cm)

Applications This floral urn motif would be a fun addition to the back of a jacket or as an embellishment for a chest pocket.

Method Use running stitch to sew 8mm roses montées onto the rim of the urn and the base, and the 4mm chaton montées onto the waist of the urn. Couch-stitch the iridescent gold and copper seed beads to fill the body of the urn, starting at the rim. String the beads so the lighter color is centered and space the couching rows close together. Couch-stitch the copper seed beads to make the scrolls at the bottom of the body, and the upper scrolls below the waist of the urn. Use matte gold flat sequins and sequins on a running stitch to sew down the lower scrolls. Stitch from the base upward. Once the urn is finished, compose a floral arrangement with the odd beads and other objects, sewing these down with a running stitch.

FEATHER

Embellishments

19	10g	10g	10g	5g
168	106	107	108	38

Stitches

〰〰 Couching stitch

--- Running stitch

〜〜 Bouclé stitch

🔍 Enlarge pattern by 250%

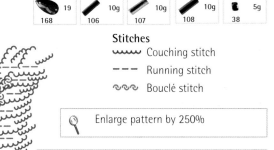

Dimensions 7 x 3³/₄ in (17.5 x 9.5cm)

Applications This glamorous feather would look graceful accenting a hat or used as a mirror-image pair to trim a V-neckline on a blouse.

Method First sew down the flat-back stones with running stitch. Begin the quill by bringing the needle up through the hole in the lower end of the stone at the tip of the feather. String enough of the gold bugle beads for the entire length of the quill and couch-stitch these down. Next, connect the rest of the stones to the quill by bringing the needle up through the holes at the ends of the stones, threading on 2 or 3 of the gold bugle beads, and couching them down. Couch-stitch the iridescent dark gold bugle beads to make the flues of the feather, and then finish the tips of the stones by bringing the needle up through the upper hole and couch-stitching 1 or 2 iridescent blue-green bugle beads in place. To create the down at the base of the flues, bouclé-stitch the iridescent dark blue seed beads using 5 beads per stitch.

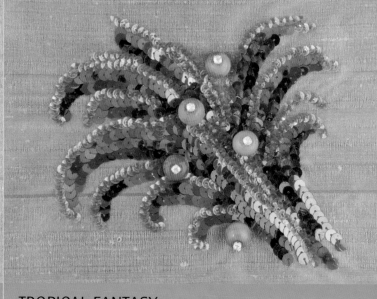

SUNFLOWER

TROPICAL FANTASY

Embellishments

	20g		3g		10g		21		105
51		95		22		158		140	

Stitches

〰〰 Couching stitch

〰 Satin stitch

- - - - Large and small beads on a backstitch

 Enlarge pattern by 274%

Embellishments

	5g		6g		5g		5		5
78		80		64		122		128	

Stitches

○ Stop stitch

○–○–○ Sequins on a running stitch

 Enlarge pattern by 290%

Dimensions 5¼ x 5¼ in
(13 x 13cm) Scales up easily.
Applications This abstract sunflower would work well used as a medallion high on the center back of a modern, kimono-style garment.
Method Fill the petals with the gold seed beads using satin stitch. The stitches near the center of the petal should be spaced closer together than those around the outer edge. Next, couch-stitch the bugle beads onto the centers of the petals and in the "W"-shaped design on the leaves. Fill in the remainder of the leaves with the green seed beads using satin stitch. For the flower center, work large and small beads on a backstitch, using the pearls and 5 of the faceted beads per stitch. Start in the center and work in a spiral pattern outward. The pearls should sit about ⅕ in (4mm) apart, so the faceted beads can form loops.

Dimensions 5¾ x 5 in (14.5 x 12cm)
Scales up relatively easily when using larger diameter sequins.
Applications This fantasy tropical frond is a playful motif that would look good peeking out of a chest pocket on an otherwise sober dinner jacket. The variation of sequin colors used here creates shading that defines the leaves.
Method Sew all of the sequins from the ends of the motif to the base using sequins on a running stitch. Sew the dark green sequins first and then the turquoise sequins in the same direction. Sew the light green cup sequins, cup-up. Finally, sew on the 12mm beads with stop stitch, using chaton montées as stop beads.

STYLIZED THISTLE

Embellishments

3g / 88	10g / 40	3g / 55	7 / 132
12 / 130	10 / 128	5g / 18	3g / 65
3g / 66	3g / 74	3g / 61	

Enlarge pattern by 325%

Stitches

wwww Couching stitch

∿∿ Satin stitch

o~o~o Sequins on a running stitch

∿∿∿ Bouclé stitch

--- Running stitch

Dimensions 5 1/2 x 5 in (14 x 12.5cm) Doesn't scale up well.

Applications As an appliqué, this abstract thistle would make a beautiful ornament for a hat, pocket, or a wide lapel on a coat.

Method Sew down the 6mm sequins, cup-up, using sequins on a running stitch, then fill between the sequins with the dark purple beads using satin stitch. Next, sew the 8mm AB chaton montées in place with the sapphire chaton montées around them, then sew the 4mm AB chaton montées into place. Couch-stitch the pink seed beads to create the borders around the chaton montées. Fill the area between the border and stones with the same seed beads, closely packed with bouclé stitch, using 3 to 5 beads per stitch. Next, work the dark green flat sequins with sequins on a running stitch, from the outside toward the middle. Do the same with the light green sequins, filling the spaces between the rows of dark sequins. Next, work the row of silver cup sequins, cup-up, starting at the middle. Sew down the silver flat sequins working from the top down. Finally, randomly space a few silver-gray seed beads using running stitch.

WEDDING FLOWER

Embellishments

3g / 61	6g / 74	6g / 85	6g / 83	120 / 139	8 / 128

Stitches

wwww Couching stitch

o~o~o Sequins on a running stitch

+H+H+H Bead mesh

Enlarge pattern by 300%

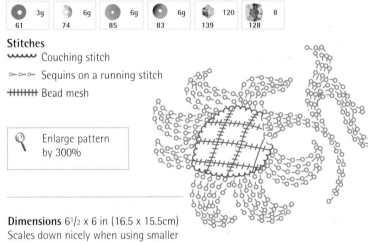

Dimensions 6 1/2 x 6 in (16.5 x 15.5cm) Scales down nicely when using smaller sequins.

Applications This large flower motif is an excellent embellishment for a mother-of-the-bride's outfit. It would be very effective on a pocket or on the shoulder of a jacket.

Method Starting at the tips of the leaves, stitch on the 3mm flat sequins using sequins on a running stitch. Fill in the rest of the leaves and the stem with the 4mm matte silver cup sequins, cup-down. Fill the petals, starting at the outside points, using a 6mm silver flat sequin and a 6mm translucent cup sequin, cup-up, on each stitch. Next, couch-stitch 4mm faceted beads around the center to make a border. Finally, sew the 4mm chaton montées to the places marked on the diagram. Make a bead mesh by connecting the chaton montées with 4mm faceted beads—use 4 beads between each chaton monté and 2 beads at the edges.

WEDDING DAISY

Embellishments

117	15g	60	5g
148	11	9	5g

Stitches

〜〜〜 Satin stitch

o–o–o– Sequins on a running stitch

〜〜〜 Bouclé stitch

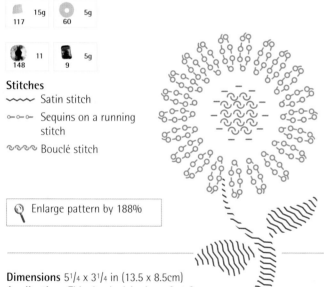

🔍 Enlarge pattern by 188%

Dimensions 5¹/₄ x 3¹/₄ in (13.5 x 8.5cm)
Applications This simple daisy is perfect for the bride whose beauty is her jewel. Use it in repetition to trim the hem of a simple empire-style gown, and then pair this with a headdress of fresh daisies.
Method Fill in the petals with sequins, working from the tips to the center, using sequins on a running stitch. Next, stitch on the circle of 8mm roses montées, and fill this circle with 6/0 iridescent gold seed beads using bouclé stitch (3 beads per stitch). Finally, fill in the stem and leaves with 11/0 two-cut beads in satin stitch.

BRIDAL BEGONIA

Embellishments

87	5g	60	3g
1	10g	26	30g

Stitches

——— Multiple beads on a backstitch

o–o–o– Sequins on a running stitch

〜〜〜 Satin stitch

〜〜〜 Bouclé stitch

🔍 Enlarge pattern by 234%

Dimensions 6 x 6 in (15.5 x 15cm)
Applications The bridal begonia is another flower that is ideal for a wedding gown. Use this lovely flower alone or in combination with other flowers to create your own bridal bouquet.
Method Outline the petals with the 6mm cup sequins, sewn cup-down using sequins on a running stitch. Work from the center of the petal tip outward and down to the center of the flower. Also work the petal emerging from the bud from tip to base. Sew on the 3mm flat sequins—these can be worked in any direction. Next, fill in the flower center with 6/0 silver seed beads using bouclé stitch, and then the stems and bud with 11/0 seed beads in satin stitch. Finally, outline the leaves with 11/0 opalescent seed beads using multiple beads on a backstitch—vary the amount of beads on the stitch as necessary.

CABBAGE ROSES

Embellishments

26	117	2	103
20g	20g	5g	30

Stitches

— Multiple beads on a backstitch

〰 Satin stitch

- - - Running stitch

///// Dangle stitch

⌒⌒⌒ Couching stitch

🔍 Enlarge pattern by 185%

Dimensions 5 x 5 in (12.5 x 12cm)
Applications The rose is a classic and well-loved flower associated with romance and weddings. This bouquet of cabbage roses would make a lovely ornament scattered in series along the hem of a bridal gown.
Method Outline the leaves with 11/0 seed beads using multiple beads on a backstitch—3 beads per stitch—and then use the same beads to fill in the outer petals of the blossoms in satin stitch. Next, fill in the inner petals with two-cut beads using satin stitch and fill the flower centers with 6/0 seed beads using running stitch. Couch-stitch two-cut beads to outline the bow knot. Finally, make the flower stems with bugle beads using dangle stitch—first 10 beads, then 12 beads, then 8 beads. Use 11/0 seed beads as the stop beads for the stems.

WEDDING POPPY

Embellishments

57	2
14g	5g

Stitches

— Backstitch

- - - Running stitch

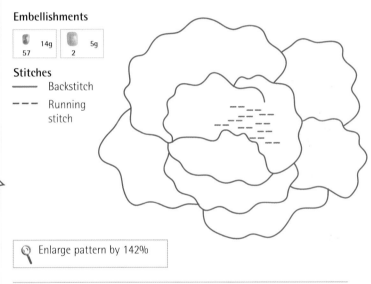

🔍 Enlarge pattern by 142%

Dimensions 4¹/₂ x 3¹/₄ in (11 x 8.5cm)
Applications This abstract poppy is simple in design and execution, and the non-directional appearance gives it great versatility. It would be excellent for filling an entire skirt or bodice.
Method Begin by sewing on the 6/0 seed beads with running stitch, randomly spaced in the area denoted on the diagram. Finally, outline all the petals with 11/0 pearlescent gray seed beads using multiple beads on a backstitch—4 beads per stitch.

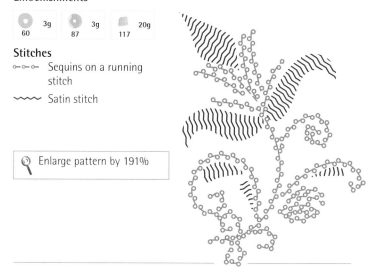

LEAVES AND BERRIES

THISTLE

Embellishments

20g		6		8	
54		160		155	
7		5			
156		154			

Stitches

—— Multiple beads on a backstitch

o Stop stitch

Embellishments

3g		3g		20g	
60		87		117	

Stitches

o-o-o- Sequins on a running stitch

∼∼∼ Satin stitch

Enlarge pattern by 191%

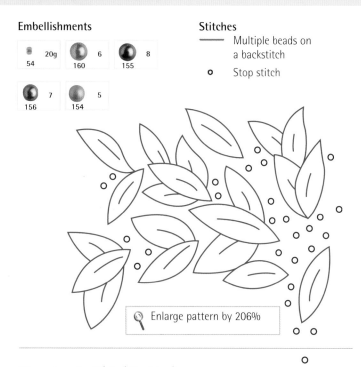

Enlarge pattern by 206%

Dimensions 6 x 5½ in (15 x 14cm)

Applications Leaves and berries are appropriate for a holiday wedding. The blue pearls used for the berries will enable you to have the traditional "something blue." This motif is equally effective scattered or spaced close together as a fill for an entire bodice.

Method Outline all of the leaves with 11/0 silver-white seed beads, using multiple beads on a backstitch—3 beads per stitch. Next, follow the diagram and photograph for the positions of the different colored pearls, and sew them using stop stitch with the 11/0 seed beads as stop beads.

Dimensions 5¼ x 3¾ in (13 x 9.5cm)

Applications This thistle is a simple but elegant motif that can be scattered over a bridal bodice or skirt or, when placed close together, would create a very special border to edge a tulle veil.

Method Sew the 3mm flat sequins with sequins on a running stitch, starting at the tips of the tendrils and working toward the stem, and then work the stem from the blossom toward the base. Fill in the bud on the lower branch, starting at the tip and working toward the stem. Next, fill in the petals of the thistle with 6mm cup sequins, working from the tips toward the base and the center lines outward. Sew these in two rows, making the second row close enough to the first to overlap. Fill in the petal on the bud with the same stitch working from tip to stem. Finally, fill in the areas reserved for satin stitch with 11/0 two-cut beads.

SILVER LILY

NOUVEAU ROSE

Embellishments

57	15g	1	5g	104	2g	132	1

129	5	85	3g	83	3g

Stitches

— Multiple beads on a backstitch

〰〰 Couching stitch

--- Running stitch

〰 Satin stitch

o–o–o Sequins on a running stitch

🔍 Enlarge pattern by 246%

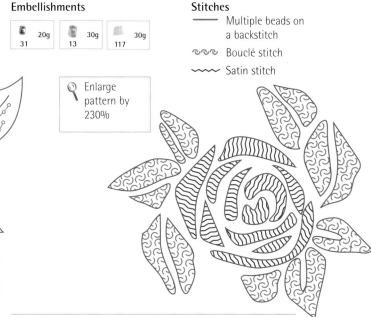

Embellishments

31	20g	13	30g	117	30g

🔍 Enlarge pattern by 230%

Stitches

— Multiple beads on a backstitch

〰〰 Bouclé stitch

〰 Satin stitch

Dimensions 6¼ x 6 in (16 x 15cm)

Applications The lily is the flower of purity and is therefore very appropriate for a wedding gown. Scatter lilies across the skirt of a wedding gown or use one in combination with other flowers to make a "bouquet" on the bodice.

Method Outline the petals with 11/0 pearlescent gray seed beads using multiple beads on a backstitch—3 beads per stitch. Finish the stem with the same seed beads in satin stitch. Create the stamens and pistils by sewing the 8mm and 4mm chaton montées into position with running stitch, and then couch-stitch the 6/0 silver seed beads and the 5mm bugle beads to make the stems. Finally, fill in the petals using sequins on a running stitch—use 1 silver sequin with 1 translucent cup sequin on top (cup-up). Begin at the tips of the petals and work down, starting at the outside and working toward the middle—cover as much of the fabric as possible.

Dimensions 7 x 5¾ in (18 x 14.5cm)

Applications This nouveau rose was inspired by the Art Nouveau movement. It would look divine scattered across the sweep of a full bridal skirt.

Method First outline all of the sections of the design with sage green seed beads using multiple beads on a backstitch—3 beads per stitch. Next, fill in the leaves with 8/0 clear seed beads in bouclé stitch. Use 3 beads per stitch and scatter the stitches closely but randomly to form a pebbly texture. Finally, follow the diagram to fill in the satin-stitch sections of the flower using two-cut beads.

GOLDEN LILY

NOSEGAY

Embellishments

151 · 2	150 · 7	97 · 4g	81 · 1g
136 · 45	86 · 3g	62 · 6g	72 · 4g

Enlarge pattern by 350%

Stitches

〰 Couching stitch

– – – Running stitch

o–o–o Sequins on a running stitch

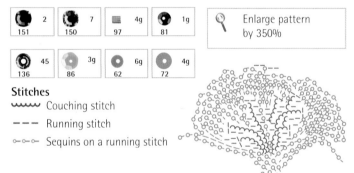

Dimensions 7 x 5¹/₂ in (18 x 14cm) Scales up easily.
Applications This blossom would be perfect for those times when a flower is needed to embellish a handbag or pocket. Made as an appliqué, it would work well as an ornament for a cloche hat.
Method Sew the topaz and smoked topaz roses montées into position using running stitch, and then couch-stitch the 2mm bugle beads as indicated. Make the center stamen by sewing down the 4mm copper cup sequins, cup-down, with sequins on a running stitch—start at the top and work downward. Use running stitch to sew the 3mm lochrosen to look randomly spaced and closer together toward the base of the flower. Use sequins on a running stitch for the 6mm translucent off-white cup sequins. Work from the center of the motif, sewing the sequins cup-up. Fill the rest of the petals with pearl beige flat sequins, starting at the top edges. The rows stop about two-thirds of the way down. From there, sew the same 3mm flat sequins randomly with running stitch to blend with the lochrosen. Use sequins on a running stitch to sew the matte gold sequins from the tips of the leaves toward the center to form the leaves and stem.

Embellishments

88 · 1g	69 · 3g	74 · 3g
128 · 7	51 · 2g	99 · 1g	22 · 5g

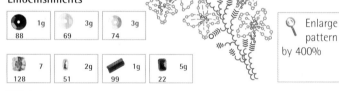

Enlarge pattern by 400%

Stitches

〰 Couching stitch

〰 Satin stitch

o–o–o Sequins on a running stitch

ᵒᵒᵒᵒ Multiple beads on a running stitch

o Stop stitch

Dimensions 5¹/₂ x 5¹/₂ in (14 x 14cm) Will not scale up easily.
Applications A sprinkling of this delicate motif across a blouse would make a superb summer design.
Method Use sequins on a running stitch to sew the 6mm orchid-pink cup sequins, cup-down, to the centers of the flower petals, starting at the outside and working inward. Use 2 to 4 sequins per petal. Leave ¹/₈ in (3–4mm) square in the flower centers. Use the same stitch to fill the rest of the petals with 4mm cup sequins, cup-up, using 1 matte silver sequin with 1 translucent pink sequin on top for each stitch. Work from the points to the centers. Sew the 4mm chaton montées into the centers and surround them with gold seed beads using multiple beads on a running stitch—9 to 11 per stitch. Make three stitches per flower center. Use bugle beads for the shanks of the flowers, using multiple beads on a running stitch—3 to 4 beads. Use green seed beads and satin stitch for the buds and bases of the flowers. For the bases, use 7 beads per stitch, then 6, then 5, then 4. For the buds, use 4 beads per stitch and then 3. For the stems, string on the number of green beads you will need to connect each flower and bud to the stem and then couch-stitch them down as marked on the diagram.

HIBISCUS

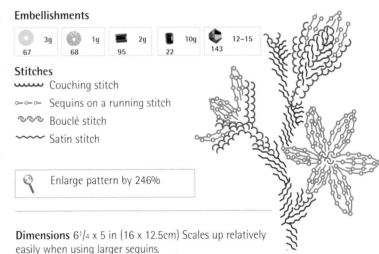

CROCUS

Embellishments

29		1g		3g		10g		40g		5g		5g
129		51		7		40		23		22		95

Stitches

- - -   Running stitch

᠊ᢌ᠊ᢌ᠊   Multiple beads on a running stitch

〜〜〜   Couching stitch

〜〜〜   Satin stitch

🔍   Enlarge pattern by 267%

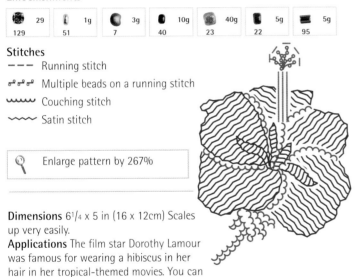

Dimensions 6¹/₄ x 5 in (16 x 12cm) Scales up very easily.

Applications The film star Dorothy Lamour was famous for wearing a hibiscus in her hair in her tropical-themed movies. You can evoke the glamour of those old movies with this flower, which scales up and down easily and makes a beautiful appliqué.

Method Use running stitch to sew down the chaton montées—5 at the end of the stamen and the rest along the stamen. Connect the 5 chaton montées to the stamen with 11/0 gold seed beads using multiple beads on a running stitch. Finish the stamen by stitching the 6/0 matte gold seed beads down with couching stitch. Work the centers of the petals with the dark purple seed beads using satin stitch. Couch-stitch the bugle beads to create the lines that separate the petals, and then fill the petals with the red-orange beads using satin stitch, couching them down in the middle of the strand. Finally, couch-stitch the green seed beads to make the stem of the flower.

Embellishments

3g		1g		2g		10g		12–15
67		68		95		22		143

Stitches

〜〜〜   Couching stitch

᠆o᠆o᠆   Sequins on a running stitch

〜〜〜   Bouclé stitch

〜〜〜   Satin stitch

🔍   Enlarge pattern by 246%

Dimensions 6¹/₄ x 5 in (16 x 12.5cm) Scales up relatively easily when using larger sequins.

Applications The crocus is one of the indications that spring has arrived. Brighten a handbag, or create a border of these crocuses along the hem of a chiffon skirt for spring.

Method Sew the pink flat sequins with sequins on a running stitch, working from the point to the center of the flower. Leave a space in the center measuring ¹/₄ x ¹/₃ in (6 x 9mm). Make the central line of sequins first. Fill in with the textured pink sequins, working from the point to the center of the flower. Sew down the bugle beads with couching stitch. To create the leaves and stems, couch-stitch the seed beads where indicated, then fill the rest of the leaves and stems with the same beads using satin stitch—sew in the directions indicated on the diagram. Finally, fill the center of the flower with the faceted beads using bouclé stitch—3 to 5 beads per stitch.

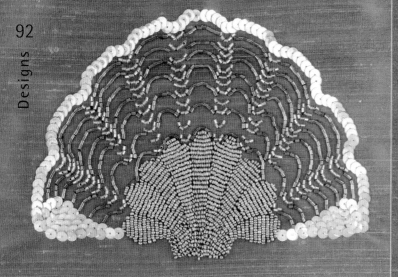

FAN SHELL

Embellishments

3g 85	3g 83	5g 97
5g 96	10g 55	10g 51

Stitches

- ○–○–○– Sequins on a running stitch
- ⌒⌒⌒ Satin stitch
- ⌇⌇⌇ Couching stitch

🔍 Enlarge pattern by 250%

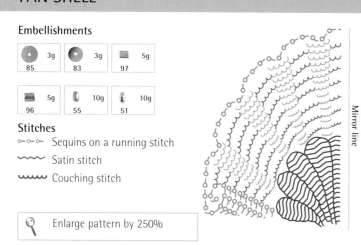

Mirror line

Dimensions 7$\frac{1}{2}$ x 5$\frac{1}{4}$ in (19 x 13cm) Scales up relatively easily.

Applications The fan shell is a fantasy design, inspired by the beauty of marine life. This design would be perfect as the shape for an evening bag. Turn it upside down as the pattern and ornament for pockets of an evening jacket.

Method Use sequins on a running stitch to work the sequins around the outer edge of the shell, working from the center at the top, down along the sides, to the bottom of the shell. Use a translucent cup sequin, cup-up, over a silver flat sequin, on each stitch. Next, couch-stitch gray bugle beads onto the brown lines indicated, using 5 to 10 beads per line. Couch-stitch the gold bugle beads first onto the light blue lines indicated on the diagram and then onto the green lines. Finish the base of the fan by sewing the gold seed beads and the silver-gray seed beads with satin stitch.

SCALLOP SHELL

Embellishments

3g 67	3g 72	1g 74
1g 69	4g 86	55 137

Stitches

- —— Multiple beads on a backstitch
- ○–○–○– Sequins on a running stitch

🔍 Enlarge pattern by 356%

Dimensions 6$\frac{1}{2}$ x 6$\frac{1}{4}$ in (16.5 x 16cm) Scales up relatively easily when using larger sequins.

Applications The scallop shell is the one in which Venus herself came ashore in Botticelli's painting. Here we have a version that will make any purse a work of art. This works well when made up as an appliqué, and can embellish a variety of garments.

Method Begin by sewing the 4mm pink flat sequins along the vertical ribs of the shell with sequins on a running stitch, working from the outside edge to the center. Make the outer edge of the shell with the 6mm translucent off-white cup sequins, sewing them cup-up with sequins on a running stitch. Work each curve separately and work from the center at the top. At the bottom of the scroll, sew the same sequins cup-down to create the scrolls, then sew the lines of the scroll working from the bottom up. Next, fill in the lines between the 6mm sequins with 4mm matte gold flat sequins, working from the bottom up, using sequins on a running stitch. Use the same stitch to complete the scroll, with a 4mm translucent pink cup sequin, cup-down, over a matte silver cup sequin on each stitch, working from the bottom up. To finish, sew the 3mm lochrosen onto the inside of the shell using multiple beads on a backstitch.

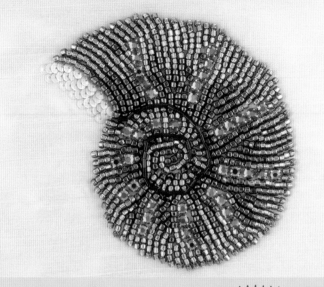

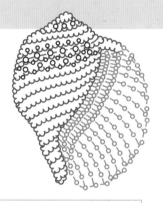

FANTASY NAUTILUS

Embellishments

▨ 39	▨ 15g	▨ 15g
149	3	5
▬ 3g	⬤ 1g	⬤ 1g
102	69	74

Stitches

〰〰 Couching stitch

--- Running stitch

○–○–○ Sequins on a running stitch

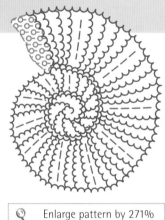

🔍 Enlarge pattern by 271%

CONCH SHELL

Embellishments

▨ 10g	▨ 10g	⬤ 3g	⬤ 1g
9	11	86	88
⬤ 6	⬤ 6	⬤ 22	▮ 30
157	148	153	51

Stitches

○ Stop stitch

〰〰 Couching stitch

○–○–○ Sequins on a running stitch

--- Running stitch

🔍 Enlarge pattern by 271%

Dimensions $5^1/_4$ x $5^1/_4$ in (13 x 13cm) Scales up easily.
Applications This fantasy nautilus shell was inspired by a mosaic in a swimming pool. The subtle shading of the different colored beads creates the relief of the shell. Use this motif as an appliqué on a beach bag, or along with the conch shell (right) to create an undersea scheme.
Method Sew down the roses montées with running stitch. Couch-stitch the 6/0 iridescent dark blue seed beads working from the opening of the shell and spiraling inward. Bring the needle up at the outside to pick up the string of beads. Work long and short strings of beads to make sure the design spirals around the shell. Use the lighter colored seed beads at the outer edge to give a three-dimensional effect. When the shell is filled, couch-stitch black bugle beads to delineate the spiral. Finally, finish the inside of the shell with pearlescent pink cup sequins on top of silver cup sequins. Sew them cup-down, using sequins on a running stitch.

Dimensions $5^1/_4$ x $4^1/_2$ in (13 x 11cm) Scales up easily.
Applications The conch shell is one of the most beautiful seashells, its highly textured outside contrasting with its pearly inside. This motif can be used in combination with other shells or by itself to trim a lapel on a jacket.
Method Make the outside of the shell by couch-stitching the 6/0 iridescent gold and copper seed beads, beginning at the point on the top of the shell. String varying numbers of the two colors onto the couching thread to mimic the texture and shading of the shell. Use sequins on a running stitch to make the inside of the shell with the translucent off-white sequins, sewn cup-down. Work from the outside edge of the shell and as you get close to the center use 2 sequins on the running stitch—an orchid-pink cup sequin with a translucent sequin over. Next, sew the 4mm and 6mm pearls into place with stop stitch, using gold seed beads as stop beads. Finally, sew the 8mm roses montées in place with running stitch.

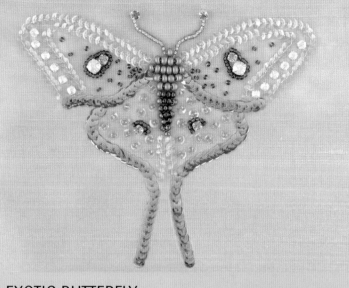

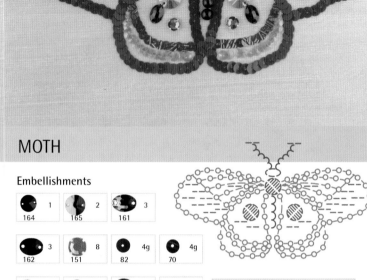

EXOTIC BUTTERFLY

Embellishments

2g	2g	12	4
79	69	128	129

2	2
130	132

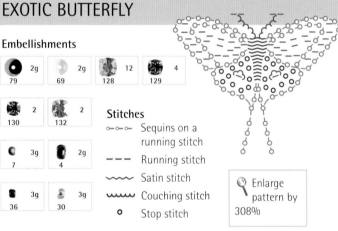

3g	2g
7	4

3g	3g
36	30

Stitches
- o–o–o Sequins on a running stitch
- – – – Running stitch
- 〜〜〜 Satin stitch
- ᨑᨑᨑ Couching stitch
- o Stop stitch

🔍 Enlarge pattern by 308%

Dimensions 5³/₄ x 5 in (14.5 x 12cm)
Applications The swallowtail butterfly is an exotic creature and this motif would make an stunning ornament for spring. Its delicate lines work best when embroidered directly onto a piece such as a pocket, blouse, or handbag.
Method Use sequins on a running stitch to outline the wings with poison green flat sequins and to sew on the pink cup sequins, cup-up. Sew down the 4mm chaton montées with running stitch: the AB ones on the outer edges of the wings, the sapphire ones at the tips of the antennae, and the padparadscha ones in the central motifs on the wings. Sew the 8mm AB chaton montées next to the 4mm padparadscha ones using running stitch. For the body, sew the 6/0 matte gold and iridescent blue seed beads into place with satin stitch. Couch-stitch the 11/0 blue seed beads around the chaton montées on the wings and the lime green seed beads along the antennae. In the lower wings, randomly scatter pink cup sequins with lime green seed beads using stop stitch, and then scatter blue seed beads in the upper wings using running stitch.

MOTH

Embellishments

1	2	3
164	165	161

3	8	4g	4g
162	151	82	70

4g	2g	4	2g
71	10	121	45

🔍 Enlarge pattern by 290%

Stitches
- – – – Running stitch
- o–o–o Sequins on a running stitch
- ᨑᨑᨑ Couching stitch

Dimensions 6³/₄ x 3¹/₂ in (17 x 9cm)
Applications The moth is a nocturnal creature, fascinated by the light of a flame. This moth would work best in the evening light of a dinner party, resting on the shoulder of a luxurious evening wrap.
Method Use sequins on a running stitch to outline the wings with the brown flat sequins and to apply the amber cup sequins and the red flat sequins to define the pattern on the wings. Next, use running stitch to sew onto the wings the 12mm sun stones, the 10 x 7mm light Colorado topaz stones, 2 of the 10 x 7mm jet stones, and the 8mm roses montées. Sew 6/0 bronze seed beads on the wings and the antennae tips with running stitch. Sew down the 12mm jet stone, a black 10 x 7mm stone for the head, and the 6mm round beads using couching stitch. Complete the antennae by couch-stitching the red seed beads.

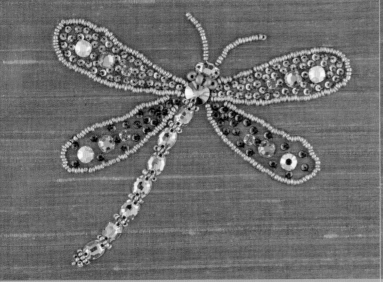

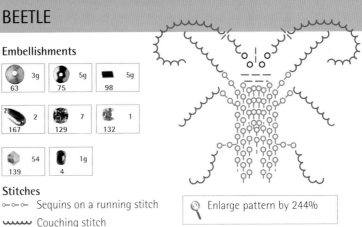

DRAGONFLY

Embellishments

161	8	163	1	51	10g
7	4–5	148	4	150	4
129	4	136	3g	137	2g

Stitches

– – – Running stitch

o‑o‑o Multiple beads on a running stitch

wwww Couching stitch

🔍 Enlarge pattern by 231%

Dimensions 5 x 3³/₄ in (12 x 9.5cm)

Applications The dragonfly was a commonly used motif in the Art Nouveau period. Its delicate lines and quick movements implied a spirit of freedom and light. Let this delightful dragonfly flit along the hem of a skirt or alight on the cuff of an evening coat.

Method Use running stitch to make the tail by sewing down 7 of the topaz flat-back stones. Use the same stitch for the head and body with the 10mm tanzanite flat-back stone and the last topaz stone. Define the tail with gold seed beads between the flat-back stones and at the tip, using multiple beads on a running stitch. Outline the wings and antennae with couch-stitched gold seed beads. Make the collar under the head with the 6/0 matte gold seed beads using multiple beads on a stitch. On the wings, sew down the 8mm AB roses montées, the 8mm topaz roses montées, and the 4mm padparadscha chaton montées, all with running stitch. Finally, using running stitch, fill in the upper wings with the tanzanite lochrosen and randomly scatter the smoked topaz lochrosen in the lower wings.

BEETLE

Embellishments

63	3g	75	5g	98	5g
167	2	129	7	132	1
139	54	4	1g		

Stitches

o‑o‑o Sequins on a running stitch

wwww Couching stitch

o Stop stitch

– – – Running stitch

🔍 Enlarge pattern by 244%

Dimensions 5¹/₂ x 4¹/₂ in (14 x 11cm)

Applications This happy little beetle isn't meant to scare anyone, just to provide some delight! Place him among some beaded flowers in a garden-themed work, perhaps on the back of a jacket or a wall hanging.

Method Create the wings on the beetle by sewing the blue cup sequins, cup-down, and then the gunmetal sequins, cup-down, with sequins on a running stitch. Outline the tops of the legs with the blue and gunmetal sequins, also cup-down, and then couch-stitch the black bugle beads to complete the legs. For the head, sew down the 18 x 10.5mm clear flat-back stones with stop stitch and the 8mm AB chaton monté with running stitch. Sew 5 4mm padparadscha chaton montées to the neck, and then sew the iridescent blue seed beads between these and the clear stones using running stitch. Finally, for each antenna, thread 3 4mm AB faceted beads, 1 padparadscha chaton monté, and approximately 22–24 4mm AB faceted beads onto a thread and couch-stitch to the fabric.

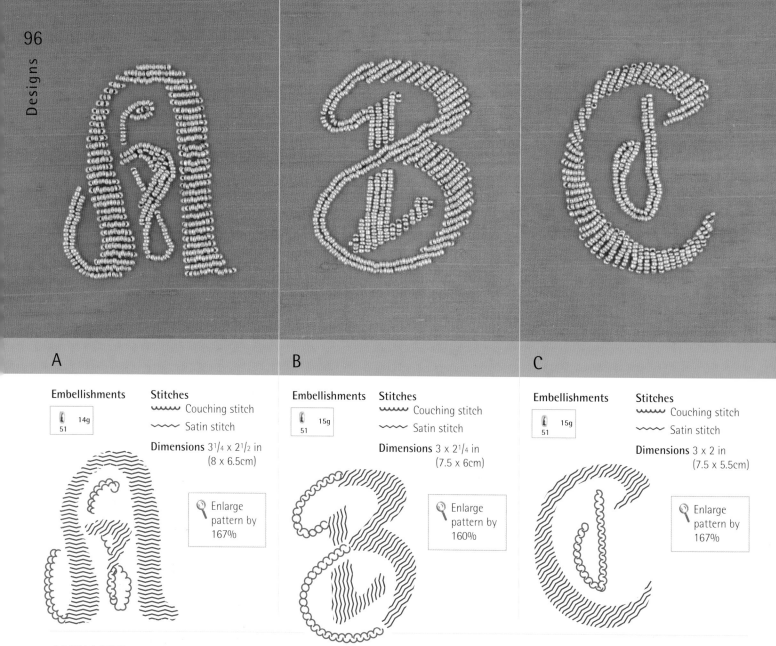

Embellishments

| 51 | 14g |

Stitches

〰〰〰 Couching stitch

〰〰 Satin stitch

Dimensions 3¼ x 2½ in (8 x 6.5cm)

🔍 Enlarge pattern by 167%

Embellishments

| 51 | 15g |

Stitches

〰〰〰 Couching stitch

〰〰 Satin stitch

Dimensions 3 x 2¼ in (7.5 x 6cm)

🔍 Enlarge pattern by 160%

Embellishments

| 51 | 15g |

Stitches

〰〰〰 Couching stitch

〰〰 Satin stitch

Dimensions 3 x 2 in (7.5 x 5.5cm)

🔍 Enlarge pattern by 167%

ALPHABET

Applications Monograms are a very effective way to personalize a project. When making something for someone you care about, the addition of their monogram makes the gift that much more special. Here is a decorative alphabet that you can use to create monograms or to spell out your message of friendship. Place a monogram on the pocket of a luxurious dressing gown for some old-time Hollywood glamor! For a more of a sparkle, you can substitute the seed beads for two-cut beads of the same size.

Method For all of the letters, it is best to begin with the curlicues. Couch-stitch these, following the photographs of the individual letters to see how they are handled. Use satin stitch to fill in the rest of the letter. When working satin stitch for the letters, start at the ends and work toward the middle, about a third of the way from each end. This way you can join the ends by gauging your spacing in the middle third of the work. The "grain" of the satin stitch does not have to match the photographs exactly—it simply has to cover the letter evenly.

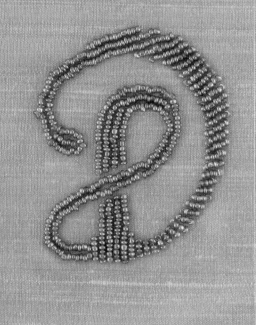

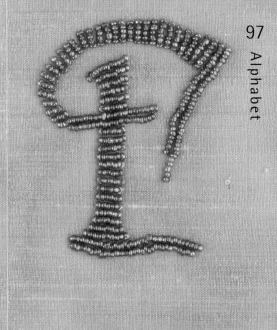

D

Embellishments

 56 15g

Stitches

〰〰 Couching stitch

〰 Satin stitch

Dimensions 3¼ x 2½ in (8 x 6.5cm)

🔍 Enlarge pattern by 170%

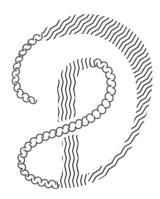

E

Embellishments

 56 16g

Stitches

〰〰 Couching stitch

〰 Satin stitch

Dimensions 3 x 2½ in (7.5 x 6.5cm)

🔍 Enlarge pattern by 163%

F

Embellishments

56 16g

Stitches

〰〰 Couching stitch

〰 Satin stitch

Dimensions 3¼ x 2½ in (8 x 6.5cm)

🔍 Enlarge pattern by 167%

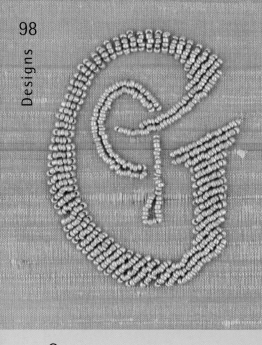
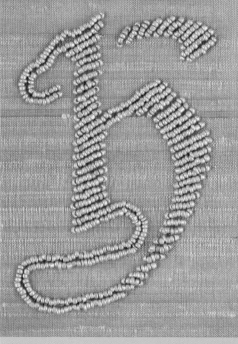
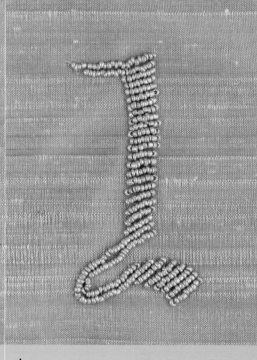

G

H

I

Embellishments

 15g
57

Stitches
〰〰〰 Couching stitch
〰〰 Satin stitch

Dimensions 3¹/₄ x 2¹/₄ in (8 x 6cm)

🔍 Enlarge pattern by 158%

Embellishments

 16g
57

Stitches
〰〰〰 Couching stitch
〰〰 Satin stitch

Dimensions 3¹/₂ x 2¹/₂ in (9 x 6.5cm)

🔍 Enlarge pattern by 184%

Embellishments

 12g
57

Stitches
〰〰〰 Couching stitch
〰〰 Satin stitch

Dimensions 3 x 1¹/₂ in (7.5 x 4cm)

🔍 Enlarge pattern by 167%

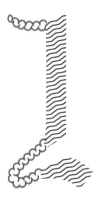

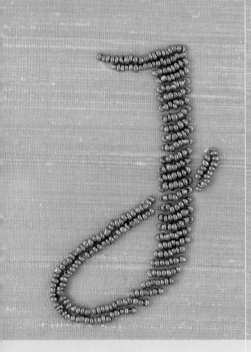

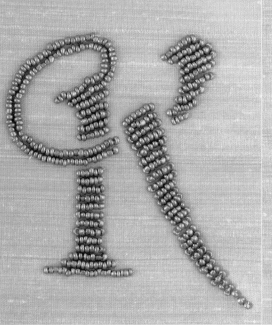

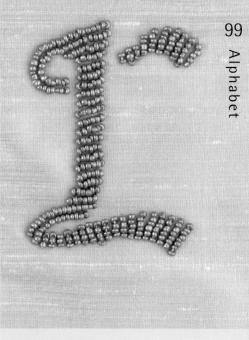

J

K

L

Embellishments

22   14g

Stitches

〰〰〰 Couching stitch

〜〜 Satin stitch

Dimensions 3¹/₂ x 2¹/₄ in (9 x 6cm)

🔍 Enlarge pattern by 188%

Embellishments

22   17g

Stitches

〰〰〰 Couching stitch

〜〜 Satin stitch

Dimensions 3¹/₂ x 3¹/₄ in (9 x 8.5cm)

🔍 Enlarge pattern by 164%

Embellishments

22   14g

Stitches

〰〰〰 Couching stitch

〜〜 Satin stitch

Dimensions 3¹/₄ x 2¹/₄ in (8 x 6cm)

🔍 Enlarge pattern by 170%

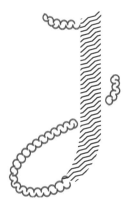

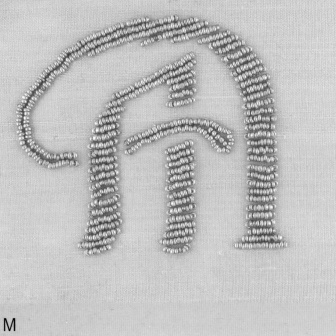

M

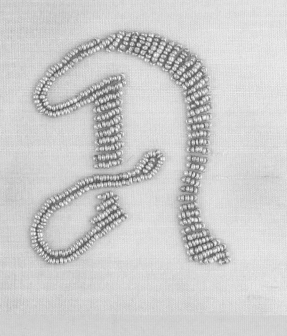

N

Embellishments

 51   16g

Stitches

 Couching stitch

〰〰 Satin stitch

Dimensions $3^3/4$ x $3^1/4$ in (9.5 x 8cm)

🔍 Enlarge pattern by 183%

Embellishments

 51   15g

Stitches

 Couching stitch

〰〰 Satin stitch

Dimensions $3^1/4$ x $2^3/4$ in (8 x 7cm)

🔍 Enlarge pattern by 140%

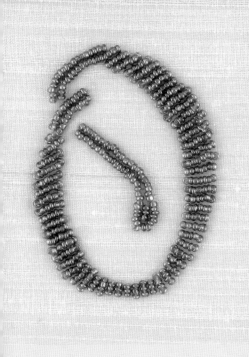

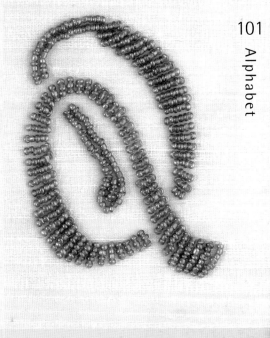

O

P

Q

Embellishments

 15g
56

Stitches
〰〰 Couching stitch

〜〜 Satin stitch

Dimensions 3$\frac{1}{4}$ x 2$\frac{1}{4}$ in (8 x 6cm)

🔍 Enlarge pattern by 167%

Embellishments

 16g
56

Stitches
〰〰 Couching stitch

〜〜 Satin stitch

Dimensions 3$\frac{1}{4}$ x 2$\frac{1}{2}$ in (8 x 6.5cm)

🔍 Enlarge pattern by 170%

Embellishments

 16g
56

Stitches
〰〰 Couching stitch

〜〜 Satin stitch

Dimensions 3$\frac{1}{4}$ x 2$\frac{1}{2}$ in (8 x 6.5cm)

🔍 Enlarge pattern by 167%

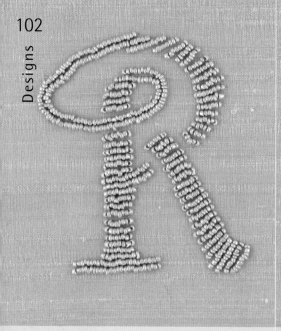

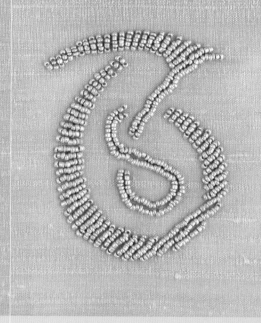

R

S

T

Embellishments

 57   16g

Stitches

〰〰〰 Couching stitch

〰〰 Satin stitch

Dimensions 3¹/₄ x 2³/₄ in (8 x 7cm)

🔍 Enlarge pattern by 178%

Embellishments

 57   15g

Stitches

〰〰〰 Couching stitch

〰〰 Satin stitch

Dimensions 3¹/₄ x 2 in (8 x 5cm)

🔍 Enlarge pattern by 167%

Embellishments

 57   17g

Stitches

〰〰〰 Couching stitch

〰〰 Satin stitch

Dimensions 3 x 2¹/₄ in (7.5 x 6cm)

🔍 Enlarge pattern by 162%

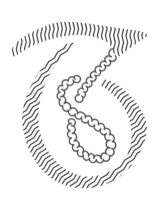

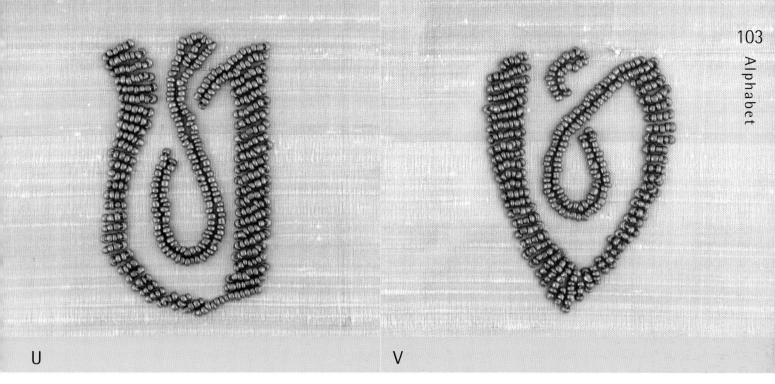

U

V

Embellishments

 15g
22

Stitches

〰〰〰 Couching stitch

〰〰 Satin stitch

Dimensions 3¹/₄ x 2 in (8 x 5cm)

 Enlarge pattern by 135%

Embellishments

 15g
22

Stitches

〰〰〰 Couching stitch

〰〰 Satin stitch

Dimensions 3 x 2¹/₄ in (7.5 x 5.5cm)

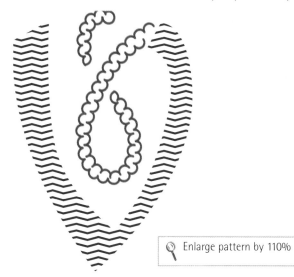

 Enlarge pattern by 110%

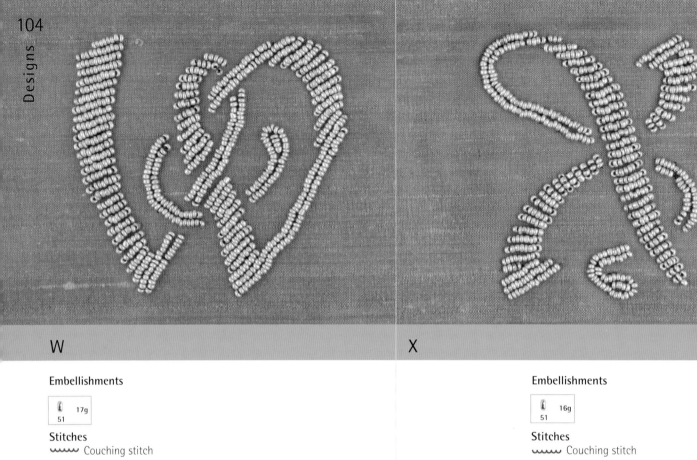

W

X

Embellishments

| 51 | 17g |

Stitches

〰〰 Couching stitch

〰 Satin stitch

Dimensions 3¹/₄ x 3¹/₄ in (8 x 8cm)

🔍 Enlarge pattern by 133%

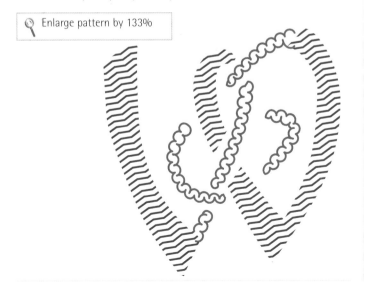

Embellishments

| 51 | 16g |

Stitches

〰〰 Couching stitch

〰 Satin stitch

Dimensions 3¹/₄ x 2¹/₂ in (8 x 6.5cm)

🔍 Enlarge pattern by 133%

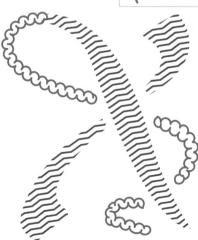

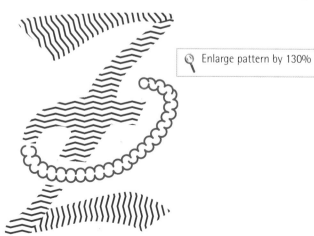

Y

Z

Embellishments

 43 | 15g

Stitches

∿∿∿ Couching stitch

∼∼∼ Satin stitch

Dimensions 3³/₄ x 2¹/₄ in
(9.5 x 6cm)

 Enlarge pattern by 109%

Embellishments

43 | 16g

Stitches

∿∿∿ Couching stitch

∼∼∼ Satin stitch

Dimensions 3¹/₄ x 2¹/₂ in (8 x 6.5cm)

 Enlarge pattern by 130%

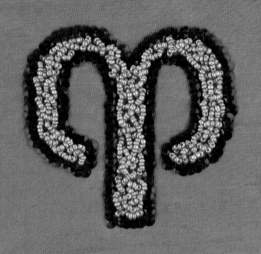

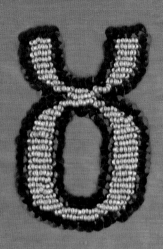

ARIES (MARCH 21 – APRIL 18)

TAURUS (APRIL 19 – MAY 20)

Embellishments

● 2g	🔵 10g
76	51

Stitches

o-o-o- Sequins on a running stitch

〰️ Bouclé stitch (7 beads per stitch)

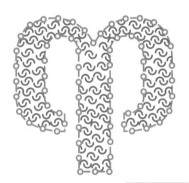

🔍 Enlarge pattern by 178%

Embellishments

● 2g	🔵 10g
76	51

Stitches

o-o-o- Sequins on a running stitch

〰️ Satin stitch

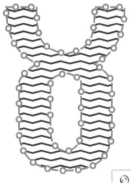

🔍 Enlarge pattern by 167%

Dimensions 3¼ x 3¼ in (8 x 8cm)

Applications Aries is energetic and takes action. Ruled by Mars, Arians are straightforward, dynamic, and filled with initiative.

Method Begin by outlining the motif with the black cup sequins, sewn cup-down, using sequins on a running stitch. Fill in the space bounded by the sequins with the seed beads using bouclé stitch—use 7 beads per stitch and pack the stitches closely to fill the entire area. Spacing is random.

Dimensions 3 x 2¼ in (7.5 x 5.5cm)

Applications Taurus is reliable and persistent. Ruled by Venus, Taureans are sensible, dependable, and responsible.

Method Outline the letter with black cup sequins, sewn cup-down, using sequins on a running stitch. Fill in the space bounded by the sequins with seed beads using satin stitch—the number of beads on the stitch should be just enough to jump across the space. Look at the photograph to see the direction of the satin stitch.

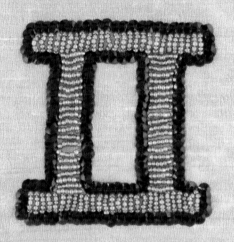

GEMINI (MAY 21 – JUNE 20)

CANCER (JUNE 21 – JULY 22)

Embellishments

 2g
76

10g
43

Stitches

 Sequins on a running stitch

〜〜 Satin stitch

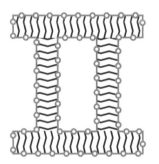

Enlarge pattern by 203%

Dimensions 3 x 3 in (7.5 x 7.5cm)

Applications Gemini is versatile and curious. People born under the sign of the twins are ruled by Mercury, making them changeable and persuasive.

Method Outline the motif with the black cup sequins, sewn cup-down, using sequins on a running stitch. Fill in the space bounded by the sequins with seed beads using satin stitch. The number of beads on the stitch should be just enough to jump across the space. The direction of the satin stitch is shown in the photograph.

Embellishments

 2g
76

10g
43

Stitches

 Sequins on a running stitch

🌿🌿🌿 Multiple beads on a stitch (worked in a braid pattern)

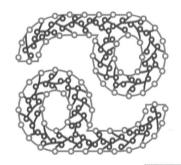

Enlarge pattern by 203%

Dimensions 3¹/₂ x 3 in (9 x 7.5cm)

Applications Cancer is intuitive and sympathetic. Those born with sun in Cancer, are ruled by the moon, making them responsive, aware, and creatures of many moods.

Method Use sequins on a running stitch to outline the motif with the black cup sequins, sewn cup-down. Fill in the space bounded by the sequins with seed beads using multiple beads on a stitch. Work the stitch in a braid pattern, making sure the braids are close enough together to fill in the space.

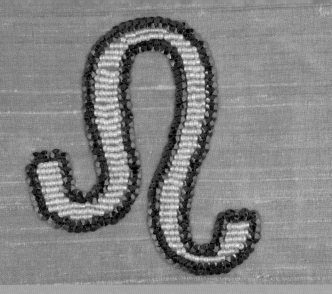

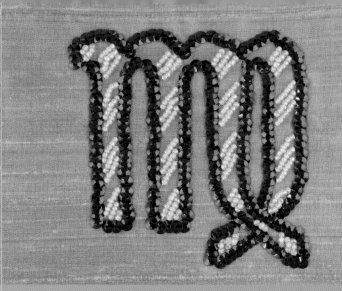

LEO (JULY 23 – AUGUST 22)

VIRGO (AUGUST 23 – SEPTEMBER 22)

Embellishments

  2g
76

25 10g

Stitches

○–○–○ Sequins on a running stitch

〜〜〜 Satin stitch

Embellishments

  2g
76

25 10g

Stitches

○–○–○ Sequins on a running stitch

〜〜〜 Satin stitch

🔍 Enlarge pattern by 158%

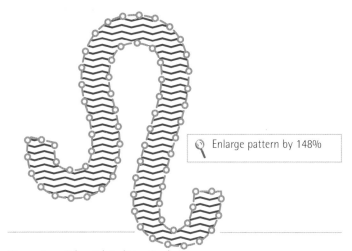

🔍 Enlarge pattern by 148%

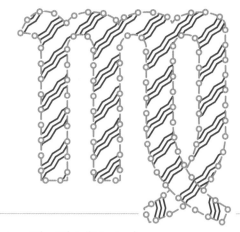

Dimensions 3³/₄ x 3¹/₂ in (9.5 x 9cm)

Applications Leo is confident and very good at self-expression. Those born under the sign of Leo are outgoing and warm, and have many friends.

Method First outline the motif with the black cup sequins, sewn cup-down, using sequins on a running stitch. Fill in the space bounded by the sequins with seed beads using satin stitch. The number of beads on a stitch should be just enough to jump across the space. Check the photograph to see the direction of the satin stitch.

Dimensions 3³/₄ x 3¹/₂ in (9.5 x 9cm)

Applications Virgo is analytical and a perfectionist. Virgoans are sharp-eyed, observant, and smart. They are always striving to improve themselves.

Method Outline the motif with the black cup sequins, sewn cup-down, using sequins on a running stitch. Fill in the space bounded by the sequins with seed beads using satin stitch—the number of beads on a stitch should be just enough to jump across the space. Look at the photograph to see the direction of the satin stitch.

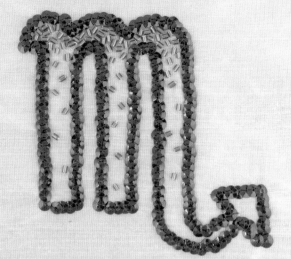

LIBRA (SEPTEMBER 23 – OCTOBER 22)

SCORPIO (OCTOBER 23 – NOVEMBER 21)

Embellishments

 2g
76

95 10g

Stitches

○—○—○ Sequins on a running stitch

〜〜〜 Satin stitch

Embellishments

2g
76

95 10g

Stitches

○—○—○ Sequins on a running stitch

――― Running stitch (random scatter)

🔍 Enlarge pattern by 164%

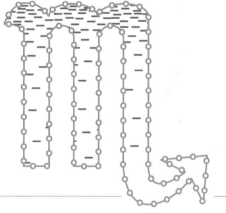

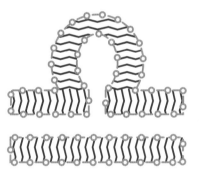

🔍 Enlarge pattern by 184%

Dimensions 3¹/₂ x 3 in (9 x 7.5cm)

Applications Libra is balanced and harmonious. Librans are refined, amiable, even-tempered, and diplomatic.

Method First outline the motif with the black cup sequins, sewn cup-down, using sequins on a running stitch. Fill in the space bounded by the sequins with bugle beads using satin stitch—the number of beads on a stitch should be just enough to jump across the space. Check the photograph to see the direction of the satin stitch.

Dimensions 3¹/₂ x 3¹/₂ in (9 x 9cm)

Applications Scorpio is passionate and intense. Ruled by Pluto, Scorpians are vibrant, magnetic, and have compelling personalities.

Method Outline the motif with the black cup sequins, sewn cup-down, using sequins on a running stitch. Fill in the space bounded by the sequins with bugle beads, using running stitch to make a random scatter. The aim is to make the scatter look even yet random.

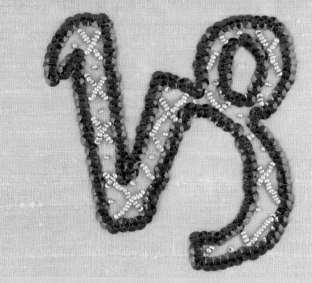

SAGITTARIUS (NOVEMBER 22 – DECEMBER 21)

CAPRICORN (DECEMBER 22 - JANUARY 19)

Embellishments

● 76	2g	🔘 51	10g

Stitches

∘–∘–∘ Sequins on a running stitch

〜〜 Satin stitch

Embellishments

● 76	2g	🔘 51	10g

Stitches

∘–∘–∘ Sequins on a running stitch

⚬⚬⚬ Multiple beads on a stitch (grid pattern)

– – – Running stitch

🔍 Enlarge pattern by 155%

🔍 Enlarge pattern by 153%

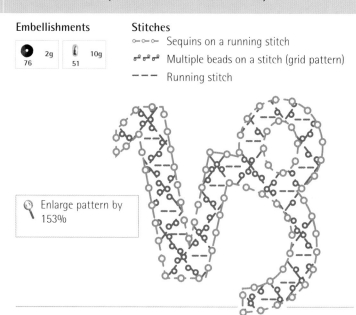

Dimensions 3¹/₄ x 2³/₄ in (8.5 x 7cm)

Applications Sagittarius is adventurous and optimistic. Ruled by Jupiter, Sagittarians are expansive, good-humored, and independent.

Method Use sequins on a running stitch to outline the motif with black cup sequins, sewing these cup-down. Fill in the space bounded by the sequins with seed beads using satin stitch—the number of beads on a stitch should be just enough to jump across the space. Check the photograph to see the direction of the satin stitch.

Dimensions 3¹/₂ x 3¹/₂ in (9 x 9cm)

Applications Capricorn is ambitious and organized. Those born under the sign of the goat are productive, responsible, and persistent.

Method First outline the motif with the black cup sequins, sewn cup-down, using sequins on a running stitch. Fill in the space bounded by the sequins with seed beads using multiple beads on a stitch, laid in a grid pattern. You can do this "by eye," or you can draw a grid on first. Once the grid is in place, you can fill in the centers of the grid with seed beads sewn on with running stitch.

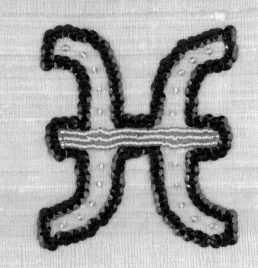

AQUARIUS (JANUARY 20 – FEBRUARY 18)

Embellishments

● 2g
76

▨ 10g
30

Stitches

o–o–o Sequins on a running stitch

∿ Satin stitch

🔍 Enlarge pattern by 179%

Dimensions 3¹/₂ x 3 in (9 x 7.5cm)
Applications Aquarius is free-thinking and original. The ruling planet is Uranus, which makes these people altruistic, charismatic, and up to date.
Method Outline the motif with the black cup sequins, sewn cup-down, using sequins on a running stitch. Fill in the space bounded by the sequins with seed beads using satin stitch—the number of beads on a stitch should be just enough to jump across the space. Look at the photograph to see the direction of the satin stitch.

PISCES (FEBRUARY 19 – MARCH 20)

Embellishments

● 2g
76

▨ 10g
30

Stitches

o–o–o Sequins on a running stitch

– – – Running stitch

∿∿∿ Couching stitch

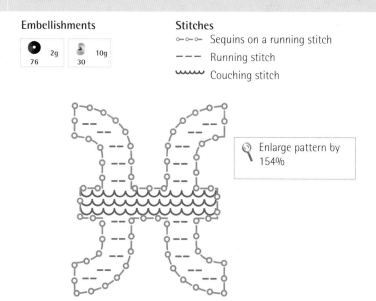

🔍 Enlarge pattern by 154%

Dimensions 3¹/₄ x 2³/₄ in (8 x 7cm)
Applications Pisces is sensitive and poetic. Pisceans are imaginative, dreamy, and people of faith.
Method Begin this motif by outlining it with the black cup sequins, sewn cup-down, using sequins on a running stitch. To fill the space bounded by the sequins, first use couching stitch to create the crossbar with seed beads, and then sew seed beads individually, in the places shown on the diagram, using running stitch.

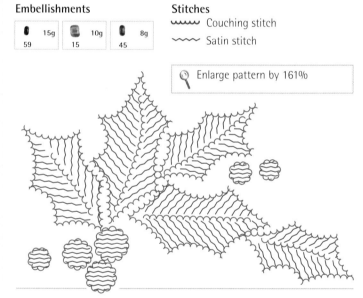

CHRISTMAS TREE

HOLLY

Embellishments

5g		20g	
30		118	

Miscellaneous
Swarovski faceted beads

Stitches

~~~ Satin stitch

--- Running stitch

Enlarge
pattern by
169%

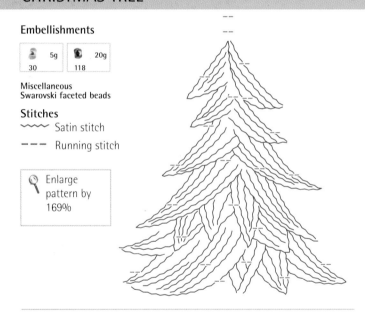

Embellishments

15g		10g		8g
59		15		45

Stitches

wwww Couching stitch

~~~ Satin stitch

Enlarge pattern by 161%

Dimensions 5¼ x 4 in (13 x 10cm)

Applications This design works well as an appliqué, which can be moved from place to place, to light up a Christmas party or dinner.

Method Work the tree in satin stitch using the two-cut dark green beads and an occasional strand of 11/0 lime green seed beads to give the tree some dimension. Follow the directions of the stitches shown in the photograph. Use running stitch to sew down the faceted beads to create the ornaments on the tree.

Dimensions 5½ x 3¾ in (14 x 9.5cm)

Applications Holly is commonly associated with Christmas. Trimming a Christmas stocking with some sprigs of holly will make it impossible to get coal in your stocking!

Method Outline the entire motif with the 11/0 black seed beads, using couching stitch. Next, fill in the holly leaves with the 8/0 green seed beads in satin stitch. Fill the berries with 11/0 red seed beads using satin stitch.

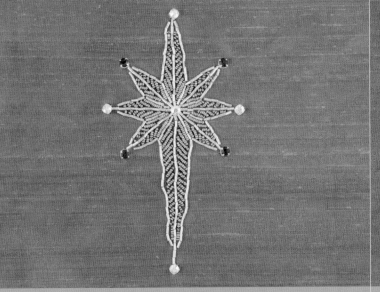

STAR OF BETHLEHEM

SILVER BELLS

Embellishments

🔩 104	15g	💊 51	20g
🐞 132	5	✳ 133	4

Stitches

〰〰〰 Couching stitch

〜〜 Satin stitch

--- Running stitch

🔍 Enlarge pattern by 201%

Embellishments

🔩 104	10g	🟫 17	5g	⬤ 80	3g
🔲 16	2g	✳ 133	7		

🔍 Enlarge pattern by 223%

Stitches

〰〰〰 Couching stitch

〜〜 Satin stitch

o–o–o– Sequins on a running stitch

--- Running stitch

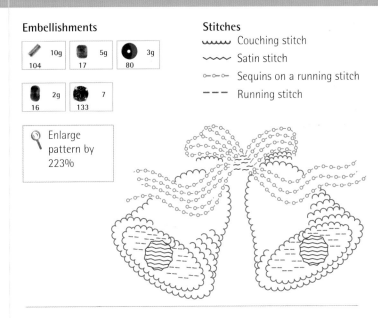

Dimensions 7 x 3³/₄ in (17.5 x 9.5cm)

Applications The Star of Bethlehem is an important symbol of Christianity at Christmastime. Let this star shine over your Christmas holiday in the form of church vestments or altarpieces.

Method Couch-stitch the outlines of the star with silver bugle beads. Next, fill the spaces in the star with the gold seed beads using satin stitch. Observe the direction of the satin stitch from the photograph. Finally, attach the AB chaton montées and the Siam chaton montées with running stitch.

Dimensions 7 x 4¹/₄ in (17.5 x 10.5cm)

Applications Silver bells are a favorite symbol of Christmastime, and this motif can become a favorite as well. Use it to decorate table linen or as a wall hanging to liven up the holiday season.

Method Couch-stitch the bugle beads to outline the bells, then satin-stitch the red seed beads to make the clappers. Make the ribbon by sewing the turquoise sequins down with sequins on a running stitch, working from the ends toward the center. Define the bow with the dark green seed beads using couching stitch, and then create shading with the same seed beads sewn with running stitch. Finally, sew on the 7 chaton montées using running stitch.

DREIDEL

HANUKKAH GELT

DREIDEL

Embellishments

▮ 59	15g	▤ 24	5g

Stitches

〜〜 Couching stitch

--- Running stitch

🔍 Enlarge pattern by 169%

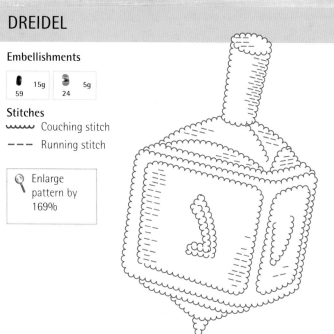

Dimensions 5¼ x 3¾ in (13.5 x 9.5cm)

Applications Dreidel is a favorite game during the Hanukkah celebrations. This design would be delightful to apply to bags that will contain the Hanukkah gelt!

Method Outline the design lines and the symbols on the dreidel with the black seed beads using couching stitch. Once these lines are in place, sew on the clear seed beads with running stitch—randomly scatter them to create the shading on the image.

HANUKKAH GELT

Embellishments

▬ 95	5g	▮ 51	10g	⬤ 73	3g

Stitches

〜〜 Satin stitch

〜〜 Couching stitch

o—o—o Sequins on a running stitch

🔍 Enlarge pattern by 136%

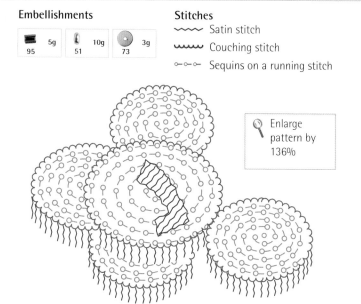

Dimensions 4 x 3¼ in (10 x 8cm)

Applications The Hanukkah gelt is won by playing the dreidel game. Embellish holiday table decorations with the Hanukkah gelt and the dreidel, to create a festive atmosphere!

Method Edge the coins with the seed beads using couching stitch, and then create the ribbed effect of the edge with bugle beads in satin stitch. Next, stitch the symbol in the central coin in satin stitch using the seed beads. Finally, fill in the surfaces of the coins with gold sequins sewn with sequins on a running stitch. Start at the edges and circle into the center.

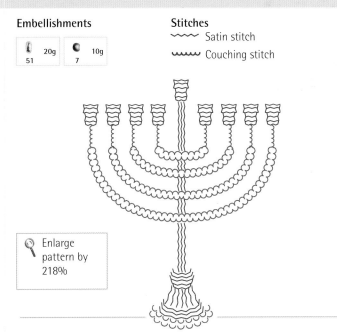

STAR OF DAVID

MENORAH

Embellishments

104   15g

Stitches

〜〜〜 Couching stitch

Embellishments

51   20g   7   10g

Stitches

〜〜〜 Satin stitch

〜〜〜 Couching stitch

Enlarge pattern by 259%

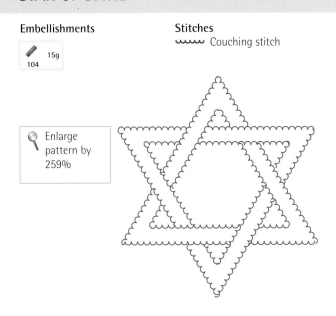

Enlarge pattern by 218%

Dimensions 5$\frac{1}{2}$ x 5$\frac{1}{2}$ in (14 x 14cm)

Applications This motif of the Star of David is not only useful for the Hanukkah celebration; it can be used any time it is considered proper. It can easily be scaled up or down.

Method The entire motif is stitched with the 5mm silver bugle beads and a couching stitch. Start at each point, and work to the inside and across. Work one section at a time. When making the stitches that couch the beads to the fabric, make sure the tension is just tight enough to hold the thread snugly, but not so tight as to cause the line of beads to buckle.

Dimensions 5$\frac{1}{2}$ x 5 in (14 x 12cm)

Applications The menorah is the symbol many people associate with Hanukkah. A beautiful use of this motif would be to embellish a tablecloth for the table where the menorah holds its place of honor.

Method Create the candleholders, the upright shaft, and the upper part of the base of the menorah with 11/0 gold seed beads using satin stitch. Next, create the arms by couch-stitching 11/0 gold seed beads. Connect these arms to the candleholders by couch-stitching the 6/0 matte gold seed beads, and then finish the base of the menorah in the same way.

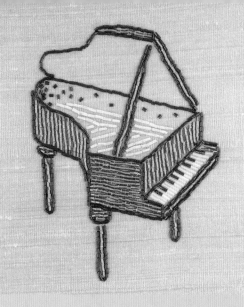

MUSICAL NOTES

PIANO

Embellishments

▬ 15g	▪ 15g		
102	116		

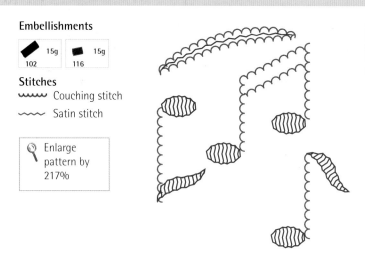

Stitches

〰〰〰 Couching stitch

〰〰 Satin stitch

🔍 Enlarge pattern by 217%

Embellishments

▬ 15g	▬ 22g	▬ 5g	▬ 10g
95	98	104	103

Stitches

〰〰〰 Couching stitch

〰〰 Satin stitch

– – – Running stitch

🍥🍥🍥 Multiple beads on a stitch

🔍 Enlarge pattern by 229%

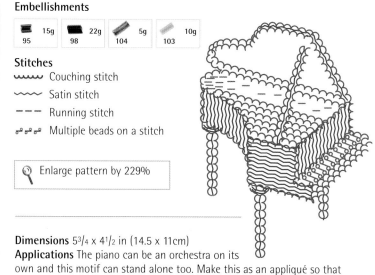

Dimensions $5^3/_4$ x $4^1/_2$ in (14.5 x 11cm)

Applications The piano can be an orchestra on its own and this motif can stand alone too. Make this as an appliqué so that you can attach it to a pocket, handbag, or pillow.

Method Outline the piano design lines with 2mm black bugle beads using couching stitch, and then fill in the outside of the piano with the 2mm copper bugle beads in satin stitch. Couch-stitch the 5mm silver bugle beads to create the strings inside the piano. Create shading inside the piano by sewing 2mm black bugle beads in a random scatter using running stitch. To make the piano keys, combine the 5mm iridescent white and the 2mm black bugle beads. There are either 2 or 3 beads to a stitch (multiple beads on a stitch), the white keys having 2 5mm white bugles, the black keys having 2 2mm black bugles and 1 5mm white bugle. Stitch these close together to mimic the pattern of black and white keys on the keyboard.

Dimensions $5^1/_4$ x $4^3/_4$ in (13 x 11.5cm)

Applications Musical notes are essential when working with a musical theme. Combine them with the instruments, or use them as an all-over pattern on a blouse for a symphony benefit.

Method Create all the straight lines of the notes, as well as the slur line, by couch-stitching the bugle beads, and then fill in the circular sections of the notes with the two-cut beads in satin stitch.

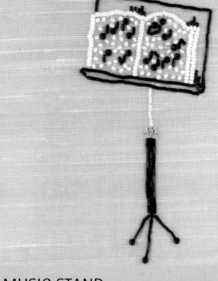

CELLO

MUSIC STAND

Embellishments

10g 116	2g 102	1g 25	5g 104	
1g 59	15g 95	3 12		

Stitches

〰️ Couching stitch

〜 Satin stitch

o Stop stitch

🔍 Enlarge pattern by 212%

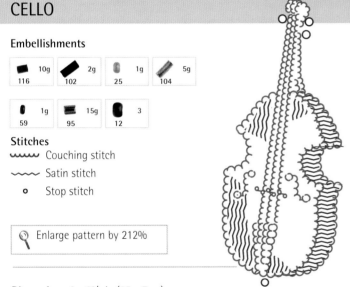

Dimensions 6 x 2³/₄ in (15 x 7cm)

Applications The cello is a mellow and warm instrument that would live well on a jacket lapel or large cuff. Combine it with the other instruments to create a musical ensemble.

Method Use couching stitch to outline the body of the cello and the tailpiece with the two-cut beads, and to outline the fingerboard with black bugle beads. Create the bridge with the iridescent clear seed beads using multiple beads on a stitch, and then couch-stitch the silver bugle beads to make the strings. Next, couch-stitch the 11/0 black seed beads to make the "F"-holes, and the copper bugle beads to make the neck of the cello. Fill in the body with the same bugle beads in satin stitch. Finally, to create the pegs, stitch the 6/0 black seed beads to the top of the neck with stop stitch, using 11/0 black seed beads as stop beads.

Embellishments

15g 102	1g 104	5g 12	5g 14	
2g 116	2g 25	2g 59		

Stitches

〰️ Couching stitch

- - - Running stitch

🔍 Enlarge pattern by 243%

Dimensions 6¹/₂ x 3¹/₄ in (16.5 x 8.5cm)

Applications The music stand completes any musically themed composition. It may stand alone or you can combine it with the instruments to create an orchestra on the back of a jacket, or for a wall hanging.

Method Couch-stitch the black bugle beads to outline the top of the music stand, the lower portion of the stand, and the feet. Use the silver bugle beads to make the silver shaft of the stand and "join" the shaft to the lower part of the stand, with three rows of 11/0 iridescent clear seed beads, using multiple beads on a stitch. Tip each foot with a 6/0 black seed bead using running stitch. Couch-stitch the 8/0 white seed beads to outline the sheet music. Make the musical notes by using the 6/0 black seed beads and stop stitch (using the 11/0 black seed beads as stop beads), and bugle beads sewn with running stitch. Use running stitch to fill in the page with randomly scattered 8/0 white seed beads and scatter two-cut beads behind the sheet music to create shadow.

TUBA

TRUMPET

Embellishments

10g 20	10g 104	3 148

Stitches

〜〜〜 Couching stitch

– – – Running stitch

ᵖ ᵖ ᵖ Multiple beads on a stitch

〜〜〜 Satin stitch

🔍 Enlarge pattern by 185%

Embellishments

🔍 Enlarge pattern by 153%

Stitches

〜〜〜 Couching stitch

〜〜〜 Satin stitch

ᵖ ᵖ ᵖ Multiple beads on a stitch

– – – Running stitch

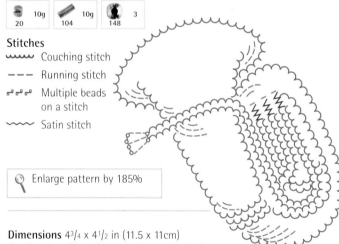

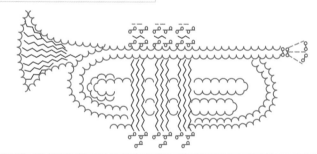

Dimensions $4^3/_4$ x $4^1/_2$ in (11.5 x 11cm)

Applications The tuba is the bass voice in the orchestra, giving weight to all of the other voices. Use this motif in combination with the other instruments, or use it solo on a jacket pocket.

Method Outline the bell of the horn, the tubes, and other fittings designated on the diagram with couch-stitched clear seed beads. Create the valves using bugle beads in satin stitch, then outline the remaining lines of the horn by couch-stitching bugle beads. Make the mouthpiece by sewing down the bugle beads with running stitch. Complete by edging the end with seed beads, using multiple beads on a stitch. Sew down the roses montées to create the buttons on the valves using a running stitch and couch-stitch the bugle beads to create the shading on the horn.

Dimensions $4^3/_4$ x $2^1/_4$ in (11.5 x 5.5cm)

Applications The trumpet is the tenor voice of the orchestra. Use this design with some of the other instruments as decoration for an evening bag.

Method Begin by couch-stitching the clear seed beads onto the designated lines and then use bugle beads to complete the valves using satin stitch. Use more of the seed beads, with multiple beads on a stitch, to finish the fittings on the valves and then couch-stitch the seed beads to create the smaller tubes on the trumpet. Couch-stitch bugle beads to outline the bell of the horn, then fill it with bugle beads in satin stitch. Finally, use running stitch to sew the faceted beads to the tops of the valves to create the buttons.

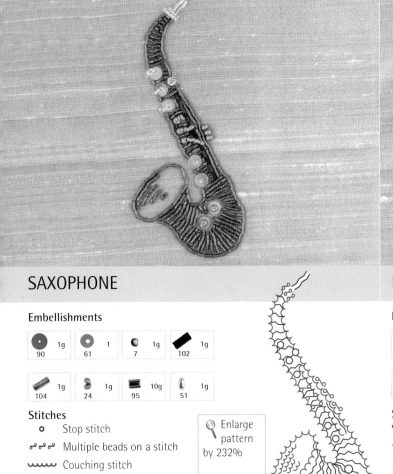

SAXOPHONE

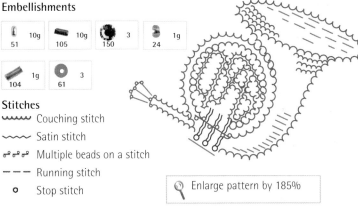

Embellishments

● 1g 90	◉ 1 61	▢ 1g 7	▬ 1g 102
▭ 1g 104	⬮ 1g 24	▤ 10g 95	◗ 1g 51

Stitches

- ○ Stop stitch
- ⬤⬤⬤ Multiple beads on a stitch
- ⌇⌇⌇ Couching stitch
- ∿∿ Satin stitch

🔍 Enlarge pattern by 232%

Dimensions 5³/₄ x 2¹/₂ in (14.5 x 6.5cm)

Applications The saxophone is a favorite with jazz musicians. Use this motif on the lapel of a funky jacket to wear to a jazz festival.

Method Stop-stitch the 7mm sequins to create the buttons. For the three top left sequins, use 5 11/0 clear seed beads as the stop beads, taking the stitch to the left of each sequin. Attach the 3mm sequin on the right in the same way, using 5 11/0 gold seed beads and taking the stitch to the right. Use a single 11/0 clear seed bead as the stop bead for the 2 middle sequins, and 1 6/0 gold seed bead and an 11/0 clear seed bead as the stop beads for the 2 sequins at the base. Couch-stitch the black bugle beads, and then create the mouthpiece using silver bugle beads in satin stitch. Make the fitting with the clear seed beads using multiple beads on a stitch. Make each of the 3 bridges to the valves with 1 6/0 gold seed bead and 5–8 11/0 gold seed beads, using multiple beads on a stitch and taking the 2 lower stitches over the black bugle beads. Couch-stitch the 2mm copper bugle beads to create the outline of the horn, and then fill in the entire horn with the same bugle beads in satin stitch. Work 3 6/0 gold seed beads to the right of the valves using multiple beads on a stitch.

FRENCH HORN

Embellishments

▯ 10g 51	▬ 10g 105	● 3 150	▮ 1g 24
▭ 1g 104	◉ 3 61		

Stitches

- ⌇⌇⌇ Couching stitch
- ∿∿ Satin stitch
- ⬤⬤⬤ Multiple beads on a stitch
- --- Running stitch
- ○ Stop stitch

🔍 Enlarge pattern by 185%

Dimensions 5 x 3 in (12 x 7.5cm)

Applications The French horn is the most poetic of all the brass instruments. Its plaintive voice lends depth to the orchestra. This motif would be perfect to embellish a jacket pocket, or used in combination with the other instruments for a sheet music folder.

Method Couch-stitch the gold seed beads to create the outline of the bell of the horn as well as the smaller tubes, and then make the valves with bronze bugle beads in satin stitch. Complete the valves with gold seed beads using multiple beads on a stitch. For the buttons on the valves, sew on 3 3mm sequins with stop stitch, using 11/0 gold seed beads as stop beads. Sew on the 8mm roses montées using running stitch. Make the outlines of the horn and the shading lines with couch-stitched bronze bugle beads Scatter gold seed beads for more shading using running stitch. Make the mouthpiece with silver bugle beads sewn on with a running stitch, then finish with clear seed beads using multiple beads on a stitch.

BEAD INDEX

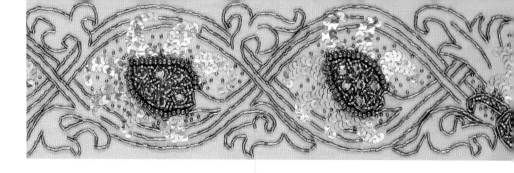

SEED BEADS

1 6/0 silver (Bridal Begonia, Silver Lily, Wedding Garland)

2 6/0 pearl finish (Bridal Rose Vine, Cabbage Roses, Wedding Poppy)

3 6/0 iridescent aquamarine (Acanthus, Fantasy Nautilus, Ribbon Lattice Border)

4 6/0 iridescent blue (Beetle, Exotic Butterfly)

5 6/0 iridescent dark blue (Acanthus, Fantasy Nautilus, Helix, Ribbon Lattice Border)

6 6/0 iridescent purple (Basketweave 1)

7 6/0 matte gold (Basic Edging Stitch, Dragonfly, Exotic Butterfly, Hibiscus, Menorah, Random Scatter: Gradient, Saxophone, Step and Repeat 2, Swag Fill)

8 6/0 gold (Abstract Owl, Neo-Gothic)

9 6/0 iridescent gold (Abstract Owl, Baroque Window, Conch Shell, Dentil Border, Floral Urn, Wands and Spears, Wedding Daisy)

10 6/0 bronze (Moth)

11 6/0 copper (Conch Shell, Floral Urn, Golden Sunflower Border, Oriental Border)

12 6/0 black (Cello, June Bug, Music Stand)

13 8/0 clear (Nouveau Rose)

14 8/0 white (Music Stand)

15 8/0 green (Holly)

16 8/0 dark green (Silver Bells)

17 8/0 red (Silver Bells)

18 8/0 pink (Peony and Scrolls, Stylized Thistle)

19 8/0 purple iridescent (Honeycomb)

20 10/0 clear (Trumpet, Tuba)

21 10/0 pearlescent white (Scallop Fill)

22 10/0 green (Alphabet: J, K, L, U, V, Crocus, Hibiscus, Ivy, Nosegay, Sunflower)

23 10/0 red-orange (Deco Scrolls, Hibiscus)

24 11/0 clear (Dreidel, French Horn, Saxophone, Swag Fill)

25 11/0 iridescent clear (Cello, Leo, Music Stand, Virgo)

26 11/0 opalescent white (Bridal Begonia, Cabbage Roses, Family Ties, Wedding Garland, Wedding Wreath)

27 11/0 translucent green (Step and Repeat 1)

28 11/0 iridescent light green (Delicate Scrolls, Ivy)

29 11/0 iridescent dark green (Celtic Lozenge, Comedy Mask, Nouveau Scroll, Peony and Scrolls)

30 11/0 lime green (Aquarius, Christmas Tree, Exotic Butterfly, Pisces)

31 11/0 sage green (Corinthian Column, Nouveau Rose)

32 11/0 iridescent aquamarine (Celtic Lozenge, Helix, Oriental Border, Patina)

33 11/0 turquoise (Deco Scrolls)

34 11/0 pearlescent blue (Harlequin)

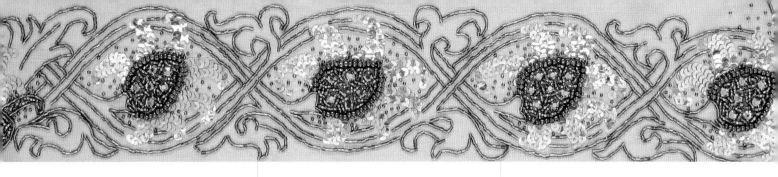

35 11/0 iridescent light blue (Step and Repeat 2, Waterfall)

36 11/0 blue (Exotic Butterfly)

37 11/0 iridescent blue (Chain Stitch Edge, Spring Scrolls)

38 11/0 iridescent dark blue (Feather)

39 11/0 purple-blue (Vines and Flowers)

40 11/0 dark purple (Baroque Lozenge, Bearded Iris, Deco Scrolls, Egg and Dart, Fountain, Hibiscus, Oriental Border, Scroll and Dart, Scroll and Poppy, Stylized Thistle)

41 11/0 iridescent purple (Baroque Lozenge, Bearded Iris, Scroll and Dart, Vines and Flowers)

42 11/0 pink-blue (Neo-Gothic)

43 11/0 iridescent pink (Alphabet: Y, Z, Cancer, Gemini)

44 11/0 orchid-pink (Tornado Border)

45 11/0 red (Holly, Moth)

46 11/0 orange (Harlequin)

47 11/0 translucent yellow (Random Scatter: Bouclé)

48 11/0 canary yellow (Deco Scrolls, Laurel Wreath, Yellow Basket)

49 11/0 copper (Abstract Owl, Celtic Lozenge, Comedy Mask, Delicate Scrolls, Egg and Dart, Fountain, Gryphon, Square Celtic Knot)

50 11/0 dark gold (Step and Repeat with Dangles)

51 11/0 gold (Alphabet: A, B, C, M, N, W, X, Aries, Arrowhead, Baroque Window, Basic Whip Stitch, Capricorn, Chain Stitch Edge, Conch Shell, Dangle Edging, Dragonfly, Egg and Dart, Fan Shell, Fountain, French Horn, Hanukkah Gelt, Hibiscus, Menorah, Nosegay, Pink Diadem, Round Celtic Knot, Sagittarius, Saxophone, Scroll and Dart, Star of Bethlehem, Sunflower, Taurus, Wands and Spears)

52 11/0 iridescent gold (Abstract Rosette, Arrowhead, Autumn Leaves, Celtic Lozenge, Fountain, Golden Sunflower Border, Gryphon, Scroll and Poppy, Square Celtic Knot, Tulip Border, Waves)

53 11/0 silver (Baroque Lozenge, June Bug, Pink Diadem, Quill Shell, Silver Bracket, Spring Scrolls)

54 11/0 silver-white (Bridal Rose Vine, Family Ties, Leaves and Berries, Wedding Garland)

55 11/0 silver-gray (Fan Shell, Stylized Thistle)

56 11/0 iridescent gray (Alphabet: D, E, F, O, P, Q, Corinthian Column, Patina, Tragedy Mask)

57 11/0 pearlescent gray (Alphabet: G, H, I, R, S, T, Corinthian Column, Silver Lily, Wedding Garland, Wedding Poppy, Wedding Wreath)

58 11/0 gunmetal gray (Deco Scrolls, Golden Sunflower Border, Tragedy Mask)

59 11/0 black (Cello, Dreidel, Holly, Music Stand)

SEQUINS

60 3mm pearl finish flat (Bridal Begonia, Family Ties, Thistle, Wedding Daisy, Wedding Wreath)

61 3mm silver flat (French Horn, Saxophone, Stylized Thistle, Wedding Flower)

62 3mm pearl beige flat (Delicate Scrolls, Golden Lily)

63 4mm blue cup (Beetle, Vermicelli Sequins)

64 4mm light green cup (Tropical Fantasy)

65 4mm light green flat (Stylized Thistle)

66 4mm dark green flat (Stylized Thistle)

67 4mm pink flat (Crocus, Scallop Shell)

68 4mm textured translucent pink flat (Crocus)

69 4mm translucent pearlescent pink cup (Exotic Butterfly, Fantasy Nautilus, Nosegay, Scallop Fill, Scallop Shell)

70 4mm textured red flat (Moth)

71 4mm amber cup (Moth)

72 4mm matte gold flat (Baroque Window, Floral Urn, Fountain, Golden Lily, Gryphon, Scallop Shell, Tulip Border)

73 4mm gold flat (Abstract Owl, Baroque Window, Comedy Mask, Deco Scrolls, Fountain, Golden Sunflower Border, Gryphon, Hanukkah Gelt, Neo-Gothic, Peony and Scrolls, Square Celtic Knot, Tulip Border)

74 4mm matte silver cup (Nosegay, Fantasy Nautilus, Quill Shell, Scallop Shell, Stylized Thistle, Wedding Flower)

75 4mm gunmetal gray cup (Beetle)

76 4mm black cup (Aquarius, Aries, Cancer, Capricorn, Gemini, Leo, Libra, Pisces, Sagittarius, Scorpio, Taurus, Tragedy Mask, Virgo, Wands and Spears)

77 5mm translucent green flat (Bearded Iris)

78 5mm dark green flat (Dentil Border, Neo-Gothic, Round Celtic Knot, Tropical Fantasy)

79 5mm poison green flat (Deco Scrolls, Exotic Butterfly)

80 5mm turquoise flat (June Bug, Oriental Border, Ribbon Lattice Border, Shadow Box Grid, Silver Bells, Tropical Fantasy)

81 4mm copper cup (Abstract Rosette, Comedy Mask, Delicate Scrolls, Golden Lily, Tornado Border)

82 5mm brown flat (Moth)

83 6mm silver flat (Fan Shell, Sapphire Bracelet, Silver Lily, Tragedy Mask, Wedding Flower)

84 6mm black cup (June Bug)

85 6mm translucent clear cup (Fan Shell, Silver Lily, Wedding Flower)

86 6mm translucent off-white cup (Conch Shell, Golden Lily, Gryphon, Scallop Shell, Tulip Border)

87 6mm iridescent white cup (Bridal Begonia, Bridal Rose Vine, Thistle)

88 6mm metallic orchid-pink cup (Conch Shell, Nosegay, Pink Diadem, Stylized Thistle)

89 6mm copper cup (Step and Repeat with Dangles)

90 7mm silver flat (Saxophone)

91 8 x 4mm navette-shaped holographic (Autumn Leaves)

92 9mm blue flat (Basket Weave 2, Ribbon Lattice Border)

93 9mm gold flat (Basket Weave 2, Dentil Border, Step and Repeat 2, Tulip Border)

94 9mm translucent flat (Family Ties, Wedding Wreath)

BUGLE BEADS

95 2mm copper (Cello, Crocus, Golden Sunflower Border, Hanukkah Gelt, Hibiscus, Libra, Medals, Oriental Border, Piano, Saxophone, Scorpio, Sunflower, Tulip Border)

96 2mm gold (Baroque Window, Comedy Mask, Fan Shell)

97 2mm gray (Fan Shell, Golden Lily, Quill Shell, Tragedy Mask)

98 2mm black (Beetle, Piano)

99 4mm pink (Nosegay, Swag Fill)

100 4mm light green (Brick Basket Weave)

101 4mm dark green (Brick Basket Weave)

102 4mm black (Cello, Fantasy Nautilus, Music Stand, Musical Notes, Saxophone)

103 5mm iridescent white (Cabbage Roses, Piano)

104 5mm silver (Baroque Lozenge, Baroque Window, Boxes, Cello, Dangle Edging, Family Ties, French Horn, Piano, Music Stand, Saxophone, Silver Bells, Silver Bracket, Silver Lily, Star of Bethlehem, Star of David, Trumpet, Tuba)

105 5mm bronze (French Horn)

106 6mm iridescent dark gold (Comedy Mask, Feather, Gryphon, Ivy, Neo-Gothic, Vermicelli Bugles)

107 6mm gold (Feather, Waterfall)

108 6mm iridescent blue-green (Autumn Leaves, Feather, Oriental Border, Spring Scrolls)

109 7mm bronze (Brick Basket Weave)

110 10mm copper twisted (Step and Repeat with Dangles)

111 11mm red (Shadow Box Grid)

112 22mm bright gold (Comedy Mask)

113 29mm sapphire (Tragedy Mask)

TWO-CUT BEADS

114 2mm gold (Random Scatter: Even)

115 10/0 iridescent brown (Oriental Border)

116 10/0 black (Cello, Music Stand, Musical Notes)

117 11/0 pearl white (Bridal Rose Vine, Cabbage Roses, Family Ties, Nouveau Rose, Thistle, Wedding Daisy, Wedding Garland, Wedding Wreath)

118 11/0 dark green (Christmas Tree)

119 11/0 black (June Bug)

ROUND BEADS

120 6mm iridescent purple (Step and Repeat 1)

121 6mm black (Moth)

122 12mm coral-colored (Tropical Fantasy)

124

PEARL BEADS

 123 4mm gray (Family Ties)

124 4mm green (Diamond Row)

125 4mm pale brown (Diamond Row)

126 6mm white (Family Ties)

127 6mm gray (Family Ties)

SWAROVSKI CRYSTAL BEADS

(AB = aurore boreale effect)

CHATON MONTÉES BEADS

128 4mm AB (Exotic Butterfly, June Bug, Nosegay, Quill Shell, Scroll and Dart, Stylized Thistle, Tropical Fantasy, Wedding Flower, Wedding Garland, Wedding Wreath)

129 4mm padparadscha (Beetle, Comedy Mask, Deco Scrolls, Dragonfly, Exotic Butterfly, Gryphon, Hibiscus, June Bug, Neo-Gothic, Oriental Border, Pink Diadem, Silver Lily)

 130 4mm sapphire (Baroque Lozenge, Exotic Butterfly, Ribbon Lattice Border, Sapphire Bracelet, Spring Scrolls, Stylized Thistle, Tragedy Mask, Vines and Flowers)

 131 4mm light Colorado topaz (Autumn Leaves, Floral Urn, Gryphon, Wands and Spears)

 132 8mm AB (Beetle, Comedy Mask, Deco Scrolls, Exotic Butterfly, Pink Diadem, Quill Shell, Ribbon Lattice Border, Scroll and Dart, Silver Bracket, Silver Lily, Star of Bethlehem, Stylized Thistle, Wedding Garland, Wedding Wreath)

 133 8mm Siam (Round Celtic Knot, Silver Bells, Star of Bethlehem)

LOCHROSEN BEADS

 134 3mm AB (Pink Diadem)

 135 3mm padparadscha (Bearded Iris, Scroll and Poppy)

 136 3mm tanzanite (Abstract Rosette, Dragonfly, Golden Lily)

 137 3mm smoked topaz (Dragonfly, Scallop Shell)

 138 5mm smoked topaz (Ivy)

FACETED BEADS

139 4mm AB bicone (Beetle, Tragedy Mask, Wedding Flower)

140 4mm turquoise bicone (Dangle Edging, Sunflower)

141 4mm tanzanite round (Comedy Mask)

142 6mm light topaz bicone (Step and Repeat with Dangles)

143 4mm smokey quartz AB bicone (Crocus, Trumpet)

144 4mm jet AB oval (Tragedy Mask)

145 6mm light topaz round (Comedy Mask)

146 6mm jet AB round (Tragedy Mask)

147 8mm olivine round (Comedy Mask, Dangle Edging)

ROSES MONTÉES BEADS

 148 8mm AB (Conch Shell, Dragonfly, Family Ties, June Bug, Tuba, Wedding Daisy)

 149 8mm olivine (Abstract Rosette, Delicate Scrolls, Egg and Dart, Fantasy Nautilus, Golden Sunflower Border, Neo-Gothic, Oriental Border, Wands and Spears)

 150 8mm topaz (Autumn Leaves, Diamond Row, Dragonfly, French Horn, Golden Lily)

 151 8mm smoked topaz (Autumn Leaves, Diamond Row, Floral Urn, Golden Lily, Moth, Tornado Border, Tulip Border)

 152 10mm clear (Family Ties, Wedding Wreath)

SWAROVSKI PEARL BEADS

 153 4mm gold (Conch Shell)

 154 6mm white (Leaves and Berries)

 155 6mm light blue (Leaves and Berries)

 156 6mm light gray (Leaves and Berries)

 157 6mm brown (Conch Shell)

 158 6mm bronze (Sunflower)

 159 8mm night blue (Helix)

 160 8mm light green (Leaves and Berries)

FLAT-BACK BEADS

 161 10 x 7mm light Colorado topaz oval (Baroque Window, Comedy Mask, Dragonfly, Moth, Wands and Spears)

 162 10 x 7mm jet oval (Moth, Tragedy Mask)

 163 10mm tanzanite (Dragonfly, Honeycomb)

 164 12mm jet (Delicate Scrolls, Medals, Moth, Tragedy Mask)

 165 12mm sun (Abstract Owl, Moth, Wands and Spears)

 166 12mm tanzanite (Baroque Lozenge, Comedy Mask, Scroll and Dart, Spring Scrolls, Vines and Flowers)

 167 18 x 10.5mm clear tear-shaped (Beetle, Swag Fill)

 168 18 x 10.5mm olivine tear-shaped (Feather)

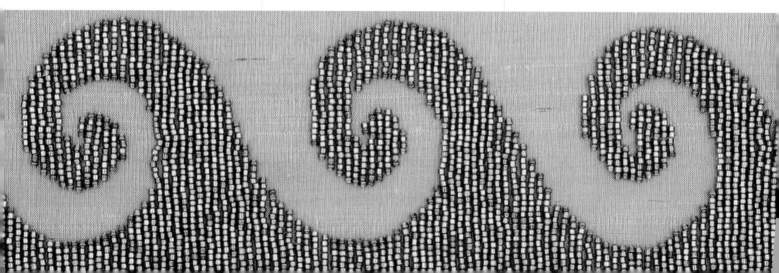

INDEX

Acknowledgments

With thanks to the companies that supplied beads for this book:

Swarovski Crystal Components

Beadcats
P.O. Box 2840
Wilsonville, Oregon
97070–2840
U.S.A.
Tel: +1 (503) 625 2323
Fax: +1 (503) 625 4329
Email: order@beadcats.com
Web: www.beadcats.com
Beadcats stocks seed beads, Czech-pressed glass beads, books, needles, and thread, and ships internationally.